A Financial System Broken by Design

How the GameStop Fiasco Exposed a Stock Market Stacked Against the Retail Investor

Nikola Biel

© **Copyright 2021 - All rights reserved.**

The content contained within this book may not be reproduced, duplicated or transmitted without direct written permission from the author or the publisher.

Under no circumstances will any blame or legal responsibility be held against the publisher, or author, for any damages, reparation, or monetary loss due to the information contained within this book, either directly or indirectly.

Legal Notice:

This book is copyright protected. It is only for personal use. You cannot amend, distribute, sell, use, quote or paraphrase any part, or the content within this book, without the consent of the author or publisher.

Disclaimer Notice:

Please note the information contained within this document is for educational and entertainment purposes only. All effort has been executed to present accurate, up to date, reliable, complete information. No warranties of any kind are declared or implied. Readers acknowledge that the author is not engaged in the rendering of legal, financial, medical or professional advice. The content within this book has been derived from various sources. Please consult a licensed professional before attempting any techniques outlined in this book.

By reading this document, the reader agrees that under no circumstances is the author responsible for any losses, direct or indirect, that are incurred as a result of the use of the information contained within this document, including, but not limited to, errors, omissions, or inaccuracies.

Table of Contents

Introduction

Part 1

Chapter 1: How the US Financial System Works

    The Major Components of the US Financial System

        The Financial Assets

        Financial Institutions

        The Financial Markets

        The Role of the Securities and Exchange Commission (SEC)

        The Federal Reserve System and Its Functions

Chapter 2: What You Should Know About the Stock Market

    What a Stock Market Is

        Understanding an Initial Public Offering Process

    The Role of a Stock Exchange

    Participants in the Stock Markets

        Stockbrokers

        Portfolio Managers

        Custodian and Depot Service Providers

        Market Makers

    Investing in Stocks

        Fundamental Analysis

        Technical Analysis

Chapter 3: Shorting a Stock—What It Means

    What Is to Short Sell a Stock?

        Short Selling in the Right Market

    What Short Interest Is

    Guilty as Charged for Market Manipulation

    Wyckoff's Operation of the Composite Operator

    The SEC Charges an Actress for Her Role in Stock Manipulation

Chapter 5: Major Short Squeezes Every Trader Should Know About
    The Piggly Wiggly® Short Squeeze
    The Volkswagen Short Squeeze
    The Tesla Short Squeeze
Part 2
Chapter 6: The Beginning of the GameStop Saga
    The History of GameStop
    Why Did Hedge Funds Short GameStop?
Chapter 7: The Major GameStop Short Squeeze
    The Role of Michael Burry in the GameStop Short Squeeze
    Wallstreetbets Investing Teachers
Chapter 8: The Ethics of the GameStop Fiasco
    Robinhood: The Uncommon Online Brokerage Firm
        How Robinhood Makes Money
        Why Robinhood Halted Buying Activity on January 28, 2020
    Ethical Questions on the Wallstreetbets Forum Members
Part 3
Chapter 9: The Hearings and What the Future Holds for the Market and Retail Investors
    Testimony by Gabriel Plotkin, CEO of Melvin Capital Management
    Kenneth Griffin's Testimony
    Keith Gill's Testimony
    CEO of Robinhood Vladimir Tenev's Testimony
Conclusion
References

Introduction

Picture this! You decide you want to invest in the stock market to build a retirement fund, buy a home, or send your children to college. The first thing you do is learn about how to invest in stocks. Once you finish that step, your next move is to find a stockbroker.

After a bit of research, you find a stockbroker charging the lowest fees or offering zero commissions. You feel that's a bargain compared to other stockbrokers. You open an account with this stockbroker and begin buying stocks. On a certain day, you wake up, and you discover that you are barred from buying a certain stock. The reason your stockbroker gives you is vague. How would you feel? Angry right?

Unfortunately, things like this can and do happen. We saw a similar situation happening recently during the GameStop short squeeze. Some retail investors lost opportunities to make money legally on the stock exchange. Just as you can get angry because of being denied an opportunity to exercise your right, I also was disturbed by what happened.

I felt angry that someone in the United States could treat others like this in a free country. Fortunately, I was able to control my anger and direct it to something that I believe will be beneficial to every retail investor and aspiring individual investor. I believe the right knowledge is vital for participating in the stock market and our advanced, though complex financial system.

If you were also angry in the past couple of months, you might have asked some of the following questions.

- How does the US financial system work?
- How do short squeezes work?
- Why did Robinhood stop trading?
- How do you tell if a stock is being shorted?
- What happens if you short a stock and it goes up?
- What did Robinhood do wrong?
- How does a hedge fund work?
- Is the stock market manipulated?

I did, and I went to investigate. Now, I am sharing what I found with you, hoping to empower and educate you to make savvy financial decisions. Most importantly, I set out to understand what really happened behind the scenes for the GameStop short squeeze to happen. I have captured my findings in this book: *A Financial System Broken by Design*. Here's what you'll find in this book.

This book is divided into three parts, Part 1, Part 2, and Part 3. The first part deals with the US financial system, short squeezes of the past, the history of GameStop, and how a stock market works. The second part focuses on the actual GameStop short squeeze to understand its mechanics. In the third part, we cover the hearings that took place and suggest a few things retail investors could do to protect themselves from major losses in the stock market. Let me give you a bit more details on what each chapter covers.

Chapter 1 goes into the details of how the US financial system works. This system consists of five major role players. These are the financial assets, financial institutions, financial markets, the Securities and Exchange Commission (SEC), and the Federal Reserve System. The reason these components exist is that there are savers and borrowers who want to connect with each other and exchange money. Money is an example of a financial asset.

However, it is not practical for each saver to find an investor who wants money. That's where financial institutions and financial markets come in. It is for this reason that we'll discuss the main financial assets that you should know. You'll become familiar with tradable securities and why they are important.

We'll go into a brief discussion of each type of financial institution, including financial intermediaries such as commercial banks and nonbank financial intermediaries. Two of the most important nonbank financial intermediaries are investment banks and hedge funds. I pay particular attention to hedge funds because they played a major role in the GameStop short squeeze. Some of what we'll talk about includes the kind of investor who is allowed to participate in a hedge fund. If you didn't know, it's not every investor who can join a hedge fund.

Human nature can be unpredictable, especially where money is involved. There is a need for regulations to ensure that people and institutions operate fairly, especially in the securities market. That's where the SEC comes in. We'll briefly explore their role in the financial system. We'll conclude Chapter 1 with a short discussion of the Federal Reserve System and its function.

In the next chapter, we shift our attention to the stock market. Our intention is to understand the role of the stock market both for businesses and investors. We cannot talk about the operations of the stock market without talking about an initial public offering or IPO. This is an important process both for the company involved and the country regarding strengthening the economy.

I am sure you have heard about the New York Stock Exchange and the Nasdaq. Do you know why they exist? If not, you'll have the answer to that question before you finish Chapter 2. A stock exchange consists of both primary and secondary markets. We'll define what these markets are and their role in our financial system. We would be remiss not to include the major role players in a stock market. One participant that I single out is market makers. We'll go through what market makers are, why they exist, and how they make money.

The final parts of Chapter 2 are focused on investing in stocks. Here, we cover the purpose of stocks. Once we complete that part, we go through the process investors follow in selecting stocks to invest in. This is where we will discuss fundamental analysis and several metrics that help you carry it out. The big idea behind fundamental analysis is to enable an investor to value a company. Thus, they can decide to either invest in it or let it pass. Many investors use fundamental analysis together with technical analysis. You use this technique to forecast the price of a security. We'll explore the various tools that you need to carry out your technical analysis and estimate a price you may enter your trade.

Stock prices always rise and fall in response to the behavior of traders and investors. Most investors tend to favor investing when stock prices are generally rising. This is what's called a bull phase. When stock prices are generally declining, generally unsophisticated investors sell their stocks or securities. In contrast, there are sophisticated investors who make money on both sides of the market. They use a process called short selling to make money on a stock whose price is declining. It's a risky operation to carry out.

We'll cover the mechanics of short selling using an example to make it clear. The reason we include short selling is that it played an immense role in the lead-up to the GameStop short squeeze. It would also help a lot when we explain the short squeeze itself. It's vital to know how short interest is measured so that you can understand it when reading on places like the Nasdaq and other sources.

One of the questions that I included above asks if the stock market is rigged. That's an important question because people may avoid investing in the stock market for fear of being manipulated or swindled out of their hard-earned money. There is a survey conducted by Bankrate that revealed interesting results. Most importantly, we include two case studies where the SEC charged a high-frequency trading company and an actress. The next chapter takes a dive into some of the major short squeezes that happened in the past. We go through the exact process that took place in the Piggly Wiggly® stock. Piggly Wiggly® was a company founded by Clarence Saunders. On a certain day, he discovered some investors on Wall Street had shorted the stock of his company. He went out of his way to teach the "smart money" a lesson, and he did. Read the whole story in Chapter 5. You'll discover the actions of the stock exchange that will probably make you question if the same thing is still happening in our modern times. Saunders finally lost the battle, having fought gallantly to save his company.

The next major short squeeze we cover is known as the Volkswagen short squeeze. We trace the short squeeze from the business relationship between Porsche and Volkswagen. Interestingly, this relationship did not end at a business level but spilled into a family relationship. Porsche actually manufactured the squeeze, and this propelled Volkswagen to the top of the world, only momentarily.

We conclude the short squeezes of the past by going through the 2020 Tesla short squeeze. Although it did not reach proportions seen on the GameStop squeeze, short sellers lost a tremendous amount of money in the process.

The GameStop short squeeze involved three main role players, GameStop itself, short sellers, and buyers. It is an ordinary practice that short sellers will short a stock if they believe it would make them money. Some short sellers, like certain hedge funds, saw an opportunity to make money on GameStop's falling stock price. Instead of starting our investigation on what happened around the time the short squeeze occurred, we step back a few strides. We actually trace the history of GameStop to understand why hedge funds were shorting their stock to unprecedented levels.

We take nearly the whole chapter investigating the history of GameStop from its inception to 2019. The most important aspect of the company we will focus on is its financial performance. This will be like doing due diligence on a company before you invest your money in it. It may feel heavy at first, but it's a study that's proven to make money for several investors. So, you are not just going to study history but also how to conduct fundamental analysis. You'll understand, in the following chapters, why certain investors chose to keep buying the stock instead of shorting it.

From this investigation and analysis, we'll answer the question of why hedge funds chose to short GameStop. That's an important conclusion because it prepares us for the next chapter.

In Chapter 7, we turn our attention to the main reason you are reading this book. I am sure you want to know what exactly led to the GameStop short squeeze. This is important because if you spot a short squeeze early, you can profit from it. However, if you short a stock, you can notice a potential short squeeze and exit your position quickly. We begin the journey by studying Michael Burry's investment strategy. We do that because one of the role players, Keith Gill, referenced him as part of his decision to keep buying GameStop stock. Burry is a hedge fund manager of his investment firm called Scion Asset Management. We trace Burry's investment style back to the time he was sharing his investment ideas on MSN. That's where he explained how he went about investing in a particular stock. The second reason we study him is that he bought millions of shares of GameStop stock when his fellow hedge fund managers were shorting it.

There is something else that Burry did at some point in 2019. He wrote three letters to the board of directors of GameStop, spelling out exactly how the company could quickly add value to its shareholders rather than destroy it as they were doing. It was a simple thing to do. It's sad that it required Burry to write three letters to explain himself. Importantly, at the time Burry wrote those letters, he was not considered an activist investor. However, he shifted out of his comfort zone and did something no one had thought he would do.

Next, we trace Keith Gill, who was posting about his GameStock investments on Wallstreetbets, a subreddit forum on Reddit. The reason we investigate his involvement is that he was identified in the media as the catalyst behind never-seen buying activity on GameStop by retail investors. He is not the only person who was posting his thoughts about GameStop on Wallstreetbets. There were a few more others like Senior_Hedgehog, whose real identity is not yet known.

The investigation would not be complete without looking into the role of Ryan Cohen, founder of a company called Chewy. Cohen bought a significant stake in GameStop and declared his holdings in around August 2020. You'll see on the GameStop stock price chart what happened from around that time. What seems to have been the tipping point is what happened on January 11, 2021. GameStop announced, on that day, the inclusion of Ryan Cohen and two of his former colleagues on the board of GameStop. However, all these things would not have happened had there been no excessive short selling of the GameStop stock.

We devote Chapter 8 to finding out if there were unethical practices and by whom. For example, during the GameStop short squeeze, on January 28, 2021, to be precise, Robinhood halted the buying of GameStop stock and other volatile stocks. This contributed to releasing the short squeeze and allowing some short sellers to exit their short positions and reduce their losses. We'll investigate this event and Robinhood itself. By the time you are done reading this chapter, you'll understand how stockbrokers actually work. That's important information for any investor or trader.

You'll also discover the existence of a private company called the Depository Trust & Clearing Corporation (DTCC). Few people know about it and its role. We'll dive into its role in Robinhood's decision to block buying of certain stocks on a fateful day in January 2021.

We won't spare some members of Wallstreetbets who seemed intent on attacking Melvin Capital Management. There are certain behaviors that were clearly untoward regarding fair play in the financial market of the United States.

In the final chapter, we shift focus to the hearings that took place in February and March 2021. We focus on only information that we didn't know or talk about in the previous chapter. The spotlight turned on Robinhood and its predominant method of generating revenue.

As you can see, this book covers a lot of ground, not only to lay bare what happened behind the scenes in the GameStop short squeeze. You also learn about the workings of our financial system as well as the stock market. Most importantly, you learn the importance of doing your due diligence when intending to invest in the stock market.

If you want helpful knowledge of our financial system, the stock market, and how the GameStop short squeeze happened, go ahead and read the rest of this book now.

Part 1

Chapter 1: How the US Financial System Works

The 2007-2008 recession convinced the world and the US citizens of the importance of a well-functioning financial system. When the system fails, many businesses fail, and thousands of people lose their livelihood. Louis Uchitelle reported in the New York Times that employers laid off around 2.6 million workers in 2008. That was the worst job loss number since 1945. When businesses collapse, the financial markets are not spared. The stock prices decline, and savings reach low levels. The finance industry, coupled with the real estate sector, contributed 21% to the gross domestic product (GDP) of the US in 2019 (Statista, 2021). GDP is a measure of a country's income. You can see that this industry is massive from the country's point of view.

Furthermore, when there are job losses, people nearing retirement are forced to keep working because their retirement savings can't support them. Sections of the economy suffer because they cannot find the raw materials they need to function properly. Every savvy investor should understand how the financial system works to protect themselves from devastating losses when things go wrong. In addition, the knowledge will help them spot investment opportunities that may not be easily seen by most.

I include this chapter so that you can understand when I explain the GameStop short squeeze. Without this foundation, you may have difficulty connecting the right dots. Currently, many people are happy to learn portions of the financial markets, such as stock investing. That's fine, but when things go wrong, such people fail to adjust and stay in control of their investments and finances. I want you to be different.

Understanding the GameStop saga, as I'll explain later, requires you to become familiar with the workings of the stock market. This requires you first to understand how the US financial system works.

The Major Components of the US Financial System

Any modern financial system, the US's included, has several components that must work together seamlessly. Because the components are interlinked, a problem in one component may affect the whole system. The US financial system consists of financial assets, financial markets, and financial institutions. There are also components that make the system work but operate outside of the system, such as the Federal Reserve regulators and the nation's citizens. Let's go over each of the components for a better understanding of the system.

The Financial Assets

An asset is anything that you own that has value. In contrast, a liability is something that you owe someone. A financial asset is an instrument of value that you own that someone else must pay you money to claim it. For example, your savings at a bank are your financial assets because they are a claim you can make against the bank. There are financial assets that you can trade and others that you cannot. Tradable assets are called securities, and you can buy and sell them in a financial market.

A financial market is a place where you can buy securities such as stocks and bonds. A good example of a financial market is the National Association of Securities Dealers Automated Quotations (Nasdaq). So, a share of Microsoft is a security because you can sell or buy it on the Nasdaq. However, a checking account isn't a security because you can't sell it.

There are many financial assets in the market. The most common we'll discuss here are money, stocks, bonds, foreign exchange, and securitized loans. Let's go over each of these important financial assets.

Money

Money is a tool used in the exchange of goods and services. It replaced the bartering system where a seller and buyer exchanged goods or services they believed had equal value. Because of increased trading between people, bartering became cumbersome. There are people who still use this system even if money is present.

When money is used as a tool of exchange and to pay debts, it is called legal tender. But it's the government that decides whether money is legal tender or not. Importantly, a given currency works within the bounds of the nation. For example, the US dollar facilitates transactions within the boundaries of the US. But other countries can use the US dollar if the government declares it a legal tender in their country, as happened in Zimbabwe during the 2008 financial crisis.

Money includes coins, paper money, and the funds in your checking account. The form that most countries currently use is called fiat money because it isn't backed up by a real asset such as gold or silver. The government controls the amount of fiat money that circulates within the financial system. When they perceive demand for more money, they print it, taking into consideration keeping inflation within a targeted range.

Inflation is the general rise in the prices of goods and services. The US targets inflation of 2% (Board of the Federal Reserve System, 2020).

Stocks

Stocks are also called equities because they represent a share of ownership of a company. Even buying a single share of a given stock gives you a certain level of ownership and the right to vote if it's a common stock.

When you buy a share of Google, you own a small part of the company. This means that you have a legal claim of the company's assets and a share of the profits. The amount of money you get quarterly (if available) due to stock ownership is called a dividend.

We'll talk more about stocks in Chapter 2 because they played a key role in the GameStop story we'll discuss later in the book. For now, we're putting the foundation together for an easier understanding of what's still to come.

Bonds

A bond is a debt security where an investor lends money to either the government or a corporation. Companies and governments issue bonds to raise funds for various purposes, such as expanding operations or building facilities. The bond is a promise that an investor will get their money back when it matures. A bond also earns a certain amount of interest.

The interest you receive is called a coupon and represents the cost of borrowing. For example, if you buy bonds worth $10,000 that mature in 30 years' time at an interest rate of 10% per year, the borrower promises to pay you $100 (10% of $10,000) annually. This means that you can get $3,000 in interest over the life of the bond if you don't reinvest the interest you receive. You can grow your money faster if you reinvest your interest because of the power of compound interest. Both your original capital and the reinvested interest will be earning interest. Furthermore, they return all your $10,000 after 30 years.

Not all bonds are long term. There are also short-term versions that mature in one year or less.

Foreign Exchange

There are many businesses that retail goods and services from outside the country. Other businesses trade goods and services they produce from raw materials produced by foreign countries. Investors have the ability to buy and sell financial assets offered by foreign businesses and governments. Now, the US dollar might not be accepted to buy these foreign goods, services, and financial assets.

As such, there's a need to convert the US to local trading currencies. That's what foreign exchange means. For example, Best Buy, an electronics retailer, might want to purchase Japanese-made televisions like Sony to sell in the US or Canada. So, they have to first convert their US dollars into Japanese yen for the trade to take place.

Large banks keep foreign currencies to help with the conversion process. As such, businesses and investors exchange their dollars with these banks so that they are able to trade in foreign countries.

Securitized Loans

Most people do not have large savings accounts to buy large items such as homes and cars for cash. To put it into perspective, the US mortgage industry was worth $11.05 trillion in 2020 (Hebron, 2020). If the US mortgage industry were a country, it would be ranked number three behind China. This tells you how big the industry is and that most Americans depend on mortgages to own homes. Financial institutions loan people money to fund these large transactions with the hope of earning interest and receiving back their original money.

Forty years ago, this was the only way that these financial institutions could earn money. But now things have changed. The government and financial institutions have created avenues to sell the loans that they make as securities. In other words, there are loans that could be traded like stocks. The process of converting loans into securities is termed securitization.

In real estate, for example, a bank would issue mortgages to successful applicants. Then, it would turn around and sell them to government-sponsored entities such as Fannie Mae and Freddie Mac or other similar firms. In turn, these entities bundle similar mortgages sourced from other banks to form what's called a mortgage-backed security (MBS). An MBS works like a bond.

An interested investor can buy or sell the MBS from a financial institution or government-backed entity. The bank that granted the original mortgage receives fees for originating the loan and collecting interest. The latter is distributed to the investor who owns the MBS.

Notice that the same financial asset can serve as an asset or a liability, depending on whose point of view we are considering. For example, when viewed from the loan provider's perspective, a car loan is an asset, yet, it is a liability from the borrower's point of view.

What we've just finished briefly discussing are the five main financial assets that make the wheels of a financial system work.

Financial Institutions

The purpose of a financial system is to match savers and borrowers. Savers are people who have excess cash beyond what they need at the moment. Not all savers have excess money. Some are driven to save for things like retirement because their employers offer the incentive to do so. Borrowers want the cash for various purposes, such as building businesses and investing in real estate. Often, the savers and borrowers are not able to meet to exchange the cash.

Suppose you have $5,000 extra cash. If there were no banks or financial institutions, where would you put it? Chances are that you'd store it somewhere in your home, isn't it? The biggest challenge that you'd face would be the risk of theft or fire. If you wanted to lend the money to someone so you earn interest, you'd have a hard time finding the right borrower. As you can see, it can be a difficult task to safely and profitably handle just $5,000. What about if you have millions of dollars? The task would become even more difficult because you'd have to find many more borrowers than when you have only $5,000.

This is where financial institutions come to the rescue by matching savers and borrowers. At the same time, you improve the chances of keeping your money safe. The Federal Deposit Insurance Corporation (FDIC) enhances the safety of your savings by up to $250,000 if using an insured bank. There's no need to purchase the insurance because you're automatically covered. However, there is a chance you might not receive your money back if you save with an uninsured bank.

Savers and borrowers connect via financial intermediaries (such as banks) and financial markets (such as the New York Stock Exchange). Suppose you want to buy a car with a loan from a bank. You're in luck because there are millions of people who've stacked their money at the bank. When you go to the bank to ask for an auto loan, the bank, after ensuring that you qualify, will grant you the cash you need. The bank isn't using their own money but cash from savers.

In return, the bank earns interest spread and fees from the loan. What do I mean by interest spread? It is the difference in interest between what the bank charges the borrower and what they pay the saver. Let's look at a simple example. The bank may charge you an annual interest rate of 5.27% (the US auto loan national average interest rate) while paying a saver 0.60% annual percentage yield (APY). The bank or financial institution would pocket 4.67% (which is 5.27% - 0.60%) to pay their employees and other business expenses. The 4.67% is what I mean by interest spread.

This way, the money flows indirectly from savers to borrowers through a financial institution. This approach to financing is called the indirect finance method. In contrast, when you buy a given company's stock, the money moves directly from the saver to the buyer. This method is called direct finance.

Overall, savers lend money to borrowers through financial institutions and financial markets either directly or indirectly. In return, the savers are paid via dividends, coupon payments, and interest payouts.

Let's now briefly go over the various financial institutions that make these funds flow seamlessly.

Financial Intermediaries

A financial intermediary connects the savers with the borrowers. Commercial banks are the major financial intermediaries. They take in deposits from the savers such as households and businesses and invest the money by making loans and buying securities. Many families rely on commercial banks when they want to buy big items such as homes, businesses, and cars.

This is understandable because few people or households have large savings accounts. For example, according to the Federal Reserve, only 61% of adults have $400 to cover emergency expenses. This attests to the fact that buying a home or a car for cash is beyond many adult Americans. So, these adults seek the financial assistance of commercial banks to buy homes and cars on loans.

Image by Gerd Altmann from Pixabay

It's not only individuals and households that depend on commercial banks. Businesses also rely on them. The money these businesses need is used to fund various projects and operations, such as covering payroll needs.

Nonbank Financial Intermediaries

There are other financial institutions that connect savers with borrowers—called nonbank financial intermediaries. They include institutions such as credit unions that take deposits and make loans. These entities offer similar services as the commercial banks, though on a smaller scale.

Another group of nonbank financial intermediaries includes insurance companies, hedge funds, mutual funds, and investment banks. These also channel funds from savers to borrowers. Let's briefly go over each of these institutions, especially the hedge funds and investment banks. They play a major role in the financial markets, a subset of the financial system we'll have a lot to say about throughout the book.

Insurance Companies

Insurance companies offer products and services that protect consumers from risk to their assets, such as cars and homes. Policyholders have a written contract with their respective insurers that stipulates the terms and conditions of the coverage. In exchange for risk coverage, the policyholders pay a premium (usually monthly).

On receiving the premiums, the insurance companies invest them to be able to cover the claims payable to shareholders. In short, you pay a premium, and the insurer multiplies it by investing it through processes such as loaning it to other businesses.

Pension Funds

There are employed people fortunate enough to contribute to an employer retirement plan, such as the 401(k) plan in the US. Many employees contribute in anticipation of accumulating enough money to retire comfortably. The challenge is that they cannot invest all their salaries into a retirement account since they must cover living expenses.

They contribute the most they can and rely on the investment to grow significantly. Some employees have employers who supplement their contributions and thus, help them grow their retirement accounts faster. The money each employee and employer contributes is pulled together into a pension fund. The fund manager invests the money in financial assets such as stocks, bonds, and mortgages.

According to Statista, pension funds grew from $16.19 trillion in 2009 to $32.22 trillion in 2019. That's a growth of 99% in just 10 years or an average growth of 9.9% per year. It is not surprising that pension funds are an important source of cash for financial securities.

Mutual Funds

A mutual fund is a pool of money sourced from various investors who are interested in growing their capital. An investor buys the shares of the fund and thereby owns a portion of the fund. The fund, in turn, invests the money in financial assets such as bonds and stocks. It is not uncommon for the mutual fund to charge a management fee. The main advantage of mutual funds is that they minimize the cost an investor would incur if they bought the individual stocks and bonds.

Mutual funds diversify their investments and thereby reduce the risk exposure to the investors. Look at this advantage in this way. If one or two firms for which the fund holds their stock go bankrupt, their impact will be minimal on the overall mutual fund's portfolio. A small retail investor who buys the stocks individually will likely suffer a significant loss when faced with the same situation. Most importantly, mutual funds offer high liquidity, which means that it is easier to access your funds in the short term.

Hedge Funds

It is important to deal with hedge funds in detail because they form an important part of the GameStop story this book talks about. Hedge funds have become popular in modern investment portfolios. A hedge fund is an investment partnership between a professional fund manager and other investors called limited partners. The fund manager and limited partners pool their money together into a fund for investment purposes.

The first hedge fund was organized by Alfred Winslow Jones in 1948 when he contributed $40,000 to a raised total of $100,000 (Chen, 2021). You may have noticed that hedge funds are a lot more like mutual funds. However, hedge funds are more aggressive and risky in their operations compared to mutual funds. It is this reason that makes them unsuited to most average investors.

Only accredited investors are allowed to form part of a hedge fund. An accredited investor is someone who earns over $200,000 a year or has a net worth of over $1 million, excluding their home. People like this arrive at such a net worth mainly after learning how to handle risks and losses.

Fund managers employ trading techniques that allow the fund to make money when the market or a stock is in the bull or bear phase. A bull phase is when the market or a stock is going up, while a bear stage signifies a market that is going down. Hedge funds' popular method of generating big returns involves buying securities on margin. This requires the fund to have access to a margin account. With this sort of account, the hedge fund borrows money from a broker and trades with it. The technique amplifies both the gains (when your trades do well) and losses (when your trades do poorly). Let me illustrate with numerical examples.

Suppose a hedge fund borrows $500,000 and adds it to their own $500,000 to buy a certain stock for $1 million. Let's further assume that the stock rises by 10%. This means that the hedge fund grows by $100,000 to $1.1 million. Now, what is the return on investment of the fund? We'll assume there are no fees or charges involved to make our calculations simple.

Return = (Total Gains / Total Investment) x 100 = ($100,000 / $500,000) x 100 =20%

Instead of getting 10%, the fund gets a 20% return on their money. This is what is meant by a concept called leverage. This is the idea of doing more with less by using someone's money to advance your financial goals. Others call using someone else's money OPM (other people's money).

Let's see what happens if the stock loses 3% of its value. The hedge fund's investment would drop by $30,000 to $970,000. Suppose the hedge fund sells after suffering this loss. Now, they'll have to return the $500,000 that they borrowed from the broker. The hedge fund would experience a loss of 6%.

Hedge funds can also invest in financial assets by using credit lines, just as you can buy a car through a loan. In this case, the fund borrows from a third party. Leveraging is a good strategy if your investment goes in your favor. Otherwise, you can suffer great losses if the investment dropped when you anticipated it to rise.

Hedge fund managers get 2% of the assets under management (AUM), whether the fund gains or loses money. So, a manager overseeing a $2 billion hedge fund can earn $40 million a year without breaking a sweat. This may be unfair to those looking from the outside because it appears the fund managers make a killing with little work. You have to get closer to these managers to appreciate whether they deserve the money or not. Better still, it's a good idea to hear what investors think about this compensation.

Corporate Finance Institute (CFI) reports that: "Renaissance Technologies, a hedge fund managed by Jim Simmons, maintained an average annual return of 71.8% between 1994 and 2015. Its worst year during the period still showed a 21% profit. Because of the high yields delivered to investors, they were willing to pay performance fees up to 44%" (CFI, n.d.). In addition, hedge fund managers earn 20% of annual profits.

The thing is that when a person is responsible for big things, they are bound to be paid more. Think about the CEO of a company. Would you say they should be paid the same salary as a middle manager? Absolutely not. The work they do is different. There is no way that their salary should even be compared.

Investment Banks

Investment banks are large financial institutions that provide advice to companies that want to create securities such as bonds and stocks. They also play a significant role in the merging of companies. Some of the big investment banks in the US include Goldman

Sachs, Morgan Stanley, and Citigroup. These financial intermediaries are also involved either as brokers or financial advisers for pension funds.

Typically, investment banks have two divisions—an advisory arm and a trading leg. Advisory divisions generate income by providing advice to their clients and getting paid a fee for the service. On the other hand, trading divisions earn commissions, the size of which depends on their performance and the agreed terms. It's likely for an investment bank to have a retail banking division that loans money directly to consumers and businesses.

However, investment banks are known for their intermediary role between a company and the financial markets. They help companies list on a stock exchange or issue additional stock to raise funds for various purposes, including expanding operations. One key task they perform is to find investors for businesses that want to sell new securities. When a company intends to create a security, it must create a prospectus that includes its financial statements. It's the role of an investment bank to scrutinize the financial statements and publish the prospectus.

Investment banking is another area where unlawful activities such as insider trading could take place. Allowing a single business to offer investment advice and facilitate a merger and acquisition provides possibilities for insider trading. True, the Sarbanes-Oxley Act (SOX) of 2002 charges companies with the task of ensuring no insider trading happens. However, we still read in the news and on the Securities Exchange Commission website about people charged with insider trading.

A case in point is that of Bryan Cohen, a former Goldman Sachs Group Inc. investment banker. S&P Global Market Intelligence reported in one of their articles on January 8, 2020, that Cohen pleaded guilty to a charge of multimillion-dollar insider trading. He had been arrested in October 2019 for exchanging nonpublic information for money in 2015. Cohen confessed that he leaked the information to a stock trader, tipping them that a certain company had approached Buffalo Wild Wings Inc. for a possible takeover. Interestingly, Cohen wasn't the first Goldman Sachs employee to be involved in insider trading. He was the third since May 2018, reported by CNBC on October 21, 2019.

The Financial Markets

The third component of the US financial system to go over is the financial markets. A market, in general, is a place where the selling and buying of goods and services take place. So, financial markets are places where traders and investors buy and sell securities such as stocks and bonds, such as the Nasdaq. The financial markets include the stock market, bond market, foreign (forex) exchange market, and commodities market.

Companies use financial markets to raise funds for different purposes. Most importantly, the financial markets simplify the process of buying and selling financial assets.

Financial markets are divided into primary and secondary markets. Let's go over each of these market categories to enhance our understanding of the financial markets and how they operate. Also, we'll develop a sense of why the financial system's design doesn't necessarily promote equality to all irrespective of their financial status.

The Primary Market

The primary markets are places where securities are sold for the first time. In other words, these financial markets are where companies and governments sell new securities. That's why the primary markets are sometimes called the "new issues" markets. These markets are the favorite territory of investment banks.

They work with the security issuers to determine the price of their offering. Furthermore, the investment banks search and find investors to buy the securities when they're launched. In turn, the security issuers pay the investment bank a commission.

The takeaway for you is that in the primary markets, the investors buy securities directly from the issuer.

The Secondary Markets

Once a security is sold in the primary market, it enters the secondary market. Here, the current holders of the security sell it to other investors and traders. Often, large investors (called institutional investors) buy a substantial amount of securities through the primary market and then sell them in the secondary markets at higher prices. The secondary market is where the majority of securities transactions take place.

Anyone who wants to buy and sell securities in the secondary market must have a brokerage account. Within the secondary markets, you'll find two categories, namely, the auction and dealer market.

- **The auction market**: In the auction market, individuals and institutional investors of securities gather in one area and broadcast the prices they wish to sell and buy the securities. A conspicuous example of an auction market is the New York Stock Exchange. The selling and buying prices are called the ask and bid prices, respectively. The rationale behind this market is that it would become efficient by having the parties coming together and declaring their prices openly. In other words, the buying and selling of securities in this manner should result in mutually agreeable prices.

- **The dealer market**: Unlike in the auction market, a dealer market works without the need for investing parties to congregate in one place. Instead, the buyers and sellers connect through electronic networks.

    There are dealers who hold a large inventory of a security who buy and sell with other participants. This is another aspect of the financial system that offers some investors an advantage over others. These large inventory holders are called market makers. They buy securities at certain prices, sell them at higher prices, and pocket the spread (or the difference). We'll talk more about market makers in Chapter 2 because of the role they play in stock market investing and trading. The Nasdaq is a good example of a dealer market.

The key difference between the primary and secondary markets is the purchase prices of the securities. For example, in the primary bond market, buyers pay the face value of the bond. So, if a bond has a par value of $2,000, that's exactly what you would pay in the primary market. However, in the secondary bond market, what you pay depends on the prevailing interest rate. If the interest rate is higher than the coupon rate (interest rate of a bond), the bond's value declines. On the other hand, when the interest rate is lower, the value of the bond rises.

To trade successfully in the secondary market requires the ability to value the securities. Otherwise, you may buy worthless securities and fail to meet your investment objectives. However, the primary market doesn't need sophisticated investing skills for you to succeed. You do need to know the right people, as put succinctly by FinancialWeb when they said, "In order to get involved in the primary market, you do not need to necessarily understand how to calculate bond values, but you do need to know the right people. Most of the time, bond sales in the primary market occur between investment banks and institutional investors" (FinancialWeb, n.d.).

We can say the same about the stock market, can't we? It seems knowing the right people opens the gates to access securities at advantageous prices, especially during the listing stage of a business. This isn't something that has started in the past 50 years or recently. It might be as old as the market themselves, as you'll see in Chapter 2.

Now, the three components of the financial system discussed above do not function alone to make it effective. Two agencies that play a role in ensuring the system runs like a well-oiled machine are the Securities and Exchange Commission (SEC) and the Federal Reserve System. So, we must look at the roles of these two institutions to complete the picture of the US financial system.

The Role of the Securities and Exchange Commission (SEC)

Congress created the Securities and Exchange Commission in 1934 to regulate the securities markets. It was a strong response to the events that led to the Great Depression that triggered the formation of the SEC. It operates independently and is charged with protecting investors and ensuring a fair and orderly operation of the securities market. Furthermore, the SEC ensures that investors and the interested public have access to information pertaining to the performance of securities such as brokers, dealers, and publicly traded companies.

The SEC carries out its functions by overseeing organizations and individuals involved in the securities market. Any investor who wants a given publicly traded company's market-related information can access it through the SEC. For example, you can access registration statements and financial reports by using the SEC's Electronic Data Gathering, Analysis, and Retrieval (EDGAR) system for free.

There are five commissioners that lead the SEC, and all are appointed by the President of the United States. One of the commissioners acts as the chairman. Each commissioner's term of office lasts for five years, with a possibility for extending another 18 months while the President searches for a suitable replacement. A maximum of three commissioners can come from the same political party.

Within the SEC, six distinct divisions and 24 offices operate. Let's briefly deal with each division.

- **The Division of Corporation Finance**: This division is responsible for ensuring that investors have access to a publicly traded company's information that can affect its stock price or financial prospects. The information is meant to aid investors in making informed investment decisions either when a company issues its securities for the first time to the public or while operating in the secondary market. Also, the division helps corporations to interpret the SEC rules and forms. The Division of Corporation Finance is allowed to recommend new rules and revisions to the prevailing rules.

- **The Division of Economic and Risk Analysis**: This division was created in September 2009. It came into being to integrate financial economics and data analytics into the activities of the SEC, such as rule-making and enforcement. Amongst this division's tasks is to discover and analyze issues and trades in the securities markets.

- **The Division of Enforcement**: It was created in 1972 to run the enforcement activities from one office instead of from multiple SEC locations. Its purpose is to enforce the SEC rules and regulations. Also, anyone found to break the SEC rules may be charged with violating the federal securities laws.

- **The Division of Examinations**: This division conducts the SEC's National Examination Program to foster the execution of the SEC's mission through risk-focused strategies that, amongst others, improve compliance and monitor risk.

- **The Division of Investment Management**: There are security participants that offer investment management services to the securities market, such as exchange-traded funds and mutual funds. This division ensures that these services work according to the rules to protect the investors.

- **The Division of Trading and Markets**: In a free market, the securities market must be fair, orderly, and efficient. This division is charged with ensuring that those characteristics of the securities market are upheld all the time. It does this by regulating transfer agents, broker-dealers, stock exchanges, and other self-regulatory organizations.

The SEC is allowed to bring relevant civil cases to either the federal court or before a judge. Also, it works closely with law-enforcement agencies to deal with cases of a criminal nature. Some of the major offenses that the SEC handles include accounting fraud and insider trading.

The Federal Reserve System and Its Functions

One of the important role players in the US financial system is the Federal Reserve. It is the central bank of the US and is responsible for ensuring inflation stays within the target. The Federal Reserve also ensures that there are stable interest rates and maximum employment. Let's go over the major functions of the Fed, as it's commonly called.

- **It manages inflation**: Unmanaged inflation can get out of hand, especially since the US dollar is fiat currency. This could lead to excessive inflation and loss of jobs. The Fed helps keep inflation at around 2%. Furthermore, the Federal Reserve sets the target for the rate at which banks loan money, which in turn influences the interest rates.

    Commercial banks are required to keep a certain amount of money at the end of each day, called reserve requirements. That target is set by the Federal Reserve. Any bank that realizes they won't have enough cash on hand at the end of each day borrows the extra funds from other banks at the federal fund rate. The Fed also adjusts the interest rates to influence business growth and employment.

- **It supervises commercial banks**: The Federal Reserve System is a network of 12 Federal Reserve banks under the direction of the Board of Governors. These banks supervise and serve as banks for their respective commercial banks. Also, the Federal Reserve handles payments, sells government securities, and assists with cash management and investment functions of the US Treasury.

- **The Fed stabilizes the financial system**: The 2008 financial crisis exposed the weaknesses of the banking system. It became clear that the existing regulations were not sufficient to keep the banking systems and banks effective. The Fed came in to stabilize the financial system through the Dodd-Frank Wall Street Reform and Consumer Protection Act of 2010.

    The Fed's supervising committee stress tests each bank to ensure it has enough capital to grant loans all the time, especially during a financial crisis.

As you can see, the Federal Reserve System is an important player in the financial markets. It affects the stock and mutual funds as well as the public's loan rates. Indirectly, this institution influences your employability and your home's value.

Chapter 2: What You Should Know About the Stock Market

If you've ever dreamed about owning a company and receiving income without working hard, you'd be interested in learning about the stock market. However, many people don't want to own and run companies. There is a way to own a company without breaking a sweat, but the rewards are not as big as owning it. You do that by buying shares in a company that you believe has good future prospects. Owning a stock of a company is one good way of generating regular income. Imagine what your life would be like when receiving dividend paychecks nearly quarterly!

As stated in Chapter 1, stocks are one of the financial assets available in the US financial system. Many investors include stocks in their investment portfolios. The place where investors and traders obtain stocks is the stock market. It is vital to understand how the stock market works to become both a savvy investor and to make sense of the GameStop saga that we will discuss later.

What a Stock Market Is

Image by Anna Nekrashevich from Pexels

A stock market is a place (physical or electronic) where investors and traders buy and sell shares in stocks of publicly traded companies. In other words, a stock market is a secondary market. However, it also serves as a primary market for the issuance of new stock to the investing public. The process where a company issues new shares to the public is called an initial public offering (IPO). Before we go deeper into how the stock market works, we must look closely into an IPO for one big reason. Investment bankers play a significant role in getting a company listed as a stock in the stock market. Like we discussed earlier, investment bankers are one place where investing fraud might take place.

Understanding an Initial Public Offering Process

An IPO is a process where a private business issues new shares to the investing public. The issuing company ceases to be private and converts into a publicly traded company. The main reason companies take their companies public is to raise funds for various business reasons such as growth. Also, an IPO offers a great opportunity for the existing investors to liquidate their shares and receive cash for their holdings. It's a big change when a company transforms from private to public.

The business must go through a rigorous process of meeting the requirements of the SEC. Furthermore, the company must be ready to handle the responsibilities of public investors. Think about it. A business moves from being accountable to a handful of private investors to thousands of investors! Generally, a company should be worth around $1 billion to make the transition to a public organization.

Most companies that go public employ the services of an investment bank as an underwriter and adviser. The IPO is a five-step process that includes selecting the right investment bank, performing due diligence and doing regulatory filings, pricing the stock, stabilizing the market for the new shares, and transitioning into the secondary market. When completed, the existing private investors can sell their shares at the value of the prevailing market price. Let's briefly discuss the IPO process for a better understanding of what's involved.

The process begins when the issuing company finds and selects an investment bank to play an advisory role and to provide underwriting functions. Some of the factors used in the selection include the reputation of the investment bank, the ability of the bank to distribute the created shares to more investors, and the relationship between the issuing company and the investment bank. The investment bank brokers the connection between the stock-issuing company and the investing public.

After selection of the investment bank, the next steps are to carry out due diligence and filing with the SEC. There are various underwriting arrangements the two parties can agree on, including the following:

- A firm commitment where the underwriter buys all the shares on offer and, in turn, sells them to the public. This is advantageous to the issuing company in that they are guaranteed to raise the money they want.

- Under the best efforts arrangement, the underwriter sells the new securities to the public on behalf of the stock-issuing company. There is no guarantee that the issuing company will raise the amount of money it needs.

- In the case of an all-or-none agreement, the investment bank must sell all the shares, or the arrangement becomes null and void.

- Finally, underwriting can involve a syndicate of underwriters. Here, the IPO is managed by multiple managers. The selected investment bank serves as the lead responsible for forming the syndicate with other competent banks, and each sells a portion of the IPO shares. This arrangement is good for the lead investment bank in that they can reduce their risk exposure.

The chosen underwriter must draft several documents, such as the engagement letter that contains the reimbursement clause and the underwriting discount. Another important document to be completed is called the registration statement. Part of the information it contains should include the issuing company's financial statements, insider shareholdings, and the background of the management team. The statement is filed only after the details of the offer have been settled.

Some of the other key documentation in the IPO process is the creation of the prospectus to be issued out to prospective investors interested in buying the IPO shares. Before preparing the final prospectus, the underwriter creates a red herring document that excludes the effective date of the offer and the initial stock price. Typically, underwriters use the red herring document to market the new shares to institutional investors during roadshows that last three to four weeks. By the way, institutional investors refer to mutual funds, pensions, and insurance companies responsible for investing on behalf of other people.

The underwriter and issuing company decide on the effective date after the SEC approves the IPO. The offer price of the shares is only known a day before the effective date. Furthermore, the investing public knows the exact number of shares to be offered a day prior to the effective date. What price the shares get offered depends on factors such as the issuing company's goal, the state of the market, and the results of the roadshows as captured in an order book. An order book in the IPO process is a list of orders from investors interested in buying the shares of a company going public. Importantly, shares are often underpriced to ensure they're fully subscribed or oversubscribed.

The next step is called stabilization, where the underwriter purchases shares at or below the offer price if there's an order imbalance. This way, the underwriter influences the market price of the shares. However, the underwriter has a limited window within which to stabilize the IPO process. Twenty-five days after the IPO, the stock price reflects the prevailing market forces. At this point, the underwriter shifts their focus to providing advisory services such as valuing the stock of the issuing company and its earnings. At this point of the process, the stock is now listed on a stock exchange.

The Role of a Stock Exchange

A stock exchange is a secondary market where sellers and buyers trade on listed companies' shares. In many cases, the listed companies rarely trade on their own shares. However, they sometimes do what's called stock buybacks or issue new shares.

There are many stock exchanges both in the US and worldwide. Many of these exchanges are hooked together electronically to make the markets more efficient and highly liquid. Modern stock exchanges are regulated and run professionally to give participants confidence that their transactions would always take place timely and at fair prices. The stock exchanges in developed countries tend to be self-regulatory organizations in that they ensure regulations and standards are adhered to.

Other versions of stock exchanges are called over-the-counter types. These are not as tightly regulated as the large stock exchanges. So, it is riskier to trade shares on these platforms than on large stock exchanges. The Nasdaq is a ubiquitous example of an over-the-counter stock exchange. Fundamentally, the main role of the stock exchange is to protect investors through the promotion of equality and ethics. Ideally, this function should protect phenomena like short squeezes. Because these events happen, exchanges are not as effective as they could be.

Participants in the Stock Markets

There are various people and institutions that take part in the activities of a stock market. One of the major participants in the stock markets is investment banks. We have already covered their role earlier when discussing the IPO process. In general, the investing participants are individual investors (or retail investors), traders, and institutional investors. However, there are other role players to ensure the stock market works as well as it should.

Stockbrokers

Stockbrokers are authorized professionals who buy and sell stocks on behalf of their clients. In the US's regulations, stockbrokers are often called broker-dealers because they take part in both the agent and dealing side of the business. In other words, besides acting as middlemen for investors and traders, they also buy and sell stocks for their own account. When they represent their clients, stockbrokers act as agents while they are dealers when they trade for their own accounts.

Portfolio Managers

Portfolio managers are professionals responsible for investing their clients' money. Often, they work for institutional investors such as mutual funds and pension funds to decide, set, and implement investment strategies for the investors' money they hold.

Custodian and Depot Service Providers

Custodian and depot service providers are institutions that hold customers' securities securely to ensure they are safe from theft or loss. Together with the exchanges, they transfer shares between the respective accounts of investors or traders involved in a buy and sell transaction.

Market Makers

A market maker is a company or individual that offers quotes on both sides of a share transaction. That is, they provide a bid and an ask as well as the market size of each. To further clarify this concept, suppose that you're a market maker in the RST stock. As the trading of the stock proceeds, you notice there is a need for liquidity in the stock and an opportunity to earn some money. So, you provide a quote of $8.00–$8.05, 200 x 400. This means that you are offering to buy 200 shares of the RST stock for $8.00 and also sell 400 shares at $8.05.

Other investors or traders may buy the shares from you at $8.05 or sell to you at $8.00. In the process, you make money from the price spread, that is, the difference in price between the ask and bid. In this case, if you buy 200 shares, you'll spend $1,600, and if you sell the 400 shares, you'll receive $3,220. Therefore, your spread will bring in $1,620. Notice that the price spread is just $0.05. It may look small, but the more shares you sell, which could number in the millions per day, the more you earn.

Most modern market making relies on heavily sophisticated trading platforms for enhanced efficiency. One of the biggest market makers on the New York Stock Exchange is a company called GTS. It's an electronic market maker that uses proprietary technology to provide liquidity to the market. This business takes care of 5% of the volume of equity trades in the US every day (GTS, n.d.).

Often, market makers are brokerage firms, although an individual trader can also perform the role. The volume of share transactions that market makers carry out is so large that many individual market makers work for big institutions.

Every market maker quotes on both buy and sell orders for a guaranteed volume of shares. As soon as a buyer places an order, the market maker fulfills it by selling off their position from their inventory. Thus, market makers simplify the buying and selling of securities. If there were no market making, it's possible that there wouldn't be enough transactions and, therefore, fewer investment opportunities.

Exchanges such as the New York Stock Exchange use a specialist system instead of market making. Technically, specialists are lone market makers who have no competition with anyone. They enjoy a monopoly over the buy and sell orders of a given security or securities. Investors make bids and asks, and the specialist broadcasts the orders for the whole market to see. Furthermore, the specialist ensures that the orders are reported timely and accurately.

Other functions of the specialist include maintaining the best price for a stock, ensuring there are orders on the trading floor, and that trades are executed. Also, the specialist works out the correct opening price of a stock based on supply and demand. That's why it is possible for the opening price of a stock to differ from its previous day closing price. There may be news and events that influence the supply and demand balance of the stock in the night. The opening price should reflect these new developments when the stock exchange opens.

Investing in Stocks

The aim of investing in stocks is to multiply your capital. Everything else you do is toward achieving that objective. There are two ways of growing your capital by investing in stocks, namely, appreciation and dividend income. Appreciation occurs when you sell your stocks at higher prices than you paid. Dividends are paid out quarterly from the profits that the company you are part-owner of makes. Not all stocks pay out dividends. That's why you need to decide ahead of time what your investment objectives would be before investing.

Your investment objectives provide you with two important benefits. From your investment goals, you'll determine your risk tolerance. Only after that would you be able to select the right stocks or investing approach and decide on the appropriate investment portfolio.

There are three approaches you could use to select the appropriate stocks for your portfolio. You can either use fundamental analysis, technical analysis, or both. The method you choose will depend upon your preference. However, value investors tend to go with fundamental analysis, while short-term profit seekers like traders often opt for technical analysis. There's no reason to choose one or the other because each serves a different purpose for the investor or trader. Let's briefly go over each of these methods.

Fundamental Analysis

Image by Campaign Creators on Unsplash

There are thousands of stocks of publicly traded companies in the United States. The New York Stock Exchange and the Nasdaq host about 6,000 stocks on their platforms. Adding in all the other 11 US exchanges makes the number even higher. How do investors and traders select stocks to invest in out of so many? It's nearly impractical for an individual to study each stock over a short time and decide whether to invest in it. Therefore, there is a need for tools to help in the selection. It is here where fundamental analysis helps with choosing stocks to study deeper for investment consideration. The following metrics and factors play a role in selecting a stock using a company's fundamentals.

Liabilities

Liabilities are also called debt. Companies can take short-term or long-term debt depending on their needs the same way an individual does. Long-term liabilities include securities such as corporate bonds. Shorter-term debt that businesses rely on might be a line of credit to deal with quick cash needs such as making payroll. Liabilities are listed on the balance sheet, one of the important financial statements of a business.

Assets

In contrast to liabilities, assets represent anything that a company owns. Assets are also listed on a company's balance sheet. You'll find them listed in categories such as cash, property, and equipment. Each asset has a certain value that can change over time due to factors such as depreciation.

Equity (or Shareholders' Equity)

Shareholders' equity is what the investors in the business own. It represents the business's net worth or book value. You determine shareholders' equity by subtracting liabilities from the assets of the company. The resulting number tells you whether the business capitalized its operations mostly from debt or investors' money. The lower the number, the more debt the company has.

Earnings Per Share (EPS)

Earnings per share is the net profit that a business makes for each share outstanding. Using this metric, you can study the trend or pattern to determine if the business's profits have been growing over time or not. Earnings, by definition, means total income minus total expenses. EPS can be negative or positive. A positive EPS means that the business spent less than it earned. The opposite is also true.

Shares Outstanding

Shares outstanding refers to the number of shares that have been authorized when the company is listed on a stock exchange. These shares are actively held by both public investors and corporate insiders.

Float

A float is a measure of the shares available for buying and selling in the stock market. You work the number out by subtracting shares held by insiders from shares outstanding. The size of a float informs you about the liquidity of a business.

When institutional investors hold more float, the company might be close to reaching its growth peak. Institutional investors buy a lot of shares and often are behind the growth in the price of stocks. A lower share ownership by institutional investors coupled with strong fundamentals indicate a higher chance that the business would do well. The reason being that more institutional investors might begin to buy the shares and push the price higher.

Price-to-Earnings (P/E) Ratio

A price-to-earnings ratio compares the prevailing stock price to the recent earnings per share. In other words, a P/E ratio tells you whether a stock is overpriced or undervalued at the moment of your analysis. This is important because you can avoid paying too much for a stock and increase your chances of capital loss.

Suppose yesterday's closing price of a particular stock was $41.32 per share and the recent quarter's earnings were $2.41 a share. Its P/E is as follows.

$$\text{Price-to-Earnings Ratio} = (\$41.32 / \$2.41) = 17.15$$

This number suggests that you'll need to receive $2.41 for nearly 18 quarters to break even, excluding expenses. The number by itself means little until you compare it with those of similar companies and the industry value. However, you could still have a targeted P/E that helps you determine whether a given company is overpriced or underpriced.

A low P/E ratio (generally below 10) indicates that fewer investors are interested in the stock. As such, the stock is cheap. This does not necessarily mean that the stock is good. A high P/E ratio (usually over 25) denotes that the stock is expensive. You may want to investigate the factors behind the high stock price. Fundamental analysts often look at the trends of ranges of P/E to have a feel of the volatility of the stock. You want a stock that's more stable over time because you can predict with a higher confidence level what might happen in the near future.

Price/Earnings to Growth (PEG) Ratio

A price/earnings to growth ratio measures the relationship between the prevailing P/E ratio and expected earnings per share. It's another metric you can use to determine if a stock is overpriced, fairly priced, or overpriced.

A PEG ratio of one suggests that a stock is priced fairly. When the ratio is less than one, the company is undervalued, while a value of more than one is an indication that the business is overvalued.

Revenue

Revenue is a measure of total sales or income that a company makes. The metric by itself means little to an investor. It becomes useful when you look at it over a period of time, such as the past five years. Furthermore, you could work out the growth in revenue to determine if the company is finding ways to sell more over a period of time. Ideally, you want to invest in a company whose sales increase from one year to the next. Declining revenues suggest that the company's near future might be in doubt.

A study of revenues adds an important dimension to an investor's decision to invest in a stock. You want to be confident that the earnings you see come from revenues, not from cost-cutting short-term interventions. If you see earnings growing while revenues are declining, you know that the company is focusing on cutting costs. This might be good temporarily but is not sustainable because you can only cut costs up to a limit.

Debt-to-Equity Ratio

The debt-to-equity ratio helps investors determine how much debt a company has relative to shareholders' equity. In other words, it tells a fundamental analyst whether a company was financed mainly through debt or equity. When it is equal to one, debt balances the equity. A debt-to-equity ratio greater than one means that the company financed its operations predominantly through debt. Ideally, a company should have a debt-to-equity ratio below one. It's a sign that it financed its activities mainly through equity.

Like all the metrics discussed above, it's better to study the trend of the debt-to-equity ratios over a period of time. Such a study will help you figure out if the company maintains its financing policy or is changing towards either debt or equity. A company that relies on financing through debt will have less money to pay dividends or to expand operations.

Return-on-Equity (ROE)

Return-on-equity is a metric obtained by dividing the annual earnings by the shareholders' equity of that year. In other words, ROE indicates how effectively a company uses equity to generate earnings.

When an investor studies the ROE trend, they may find that it declines. This by itself does not mean that the company is bad. You'll need to evaluate the fundamentals mentioned above to complete your analysis of the company. If the other fundamentals are trending towards the negative, you may want to avoid buying the stock.

Keep in mind that it is easier for a smaller company to deliver large ROE than a mature business. It's tougher for a large company to grow aggressively because it has more complexity within it. So, it can take a while to see the result of a business growth initiative.

Dividend Yield Ratio

A dividend is a certain amount of money that some listed companies pay out to investors quarterly. The amount is small and some investors may see it as unimportant. A dividend yield is a percentage you obtain by dividing the annual dividend by the prevailing stock price. A dividend yield does not appear on any financial statement. You, therefore, have to calculate it.

Suppose a certain company's stock is trading at $48 a share. Furthermore, the business paid quarterly dividends of $0.32 per share. The dividend yield will be as follows.

$$\text{Dividend Yield Ratio} = (\$.032 \times 4) / \$48 = .027 \text{ or } 2.7\%$$

This number suggests that if you pay $48 for the share, your dividend yield will be 2.7% as long as you hold the stock.

Market Capitalization

Market capitalization (or market cap for short) refers to the size of the investment market that a listed company has. You obtain it by multiplying the number of shares outstanding by the existing stock price. For example, if Company A has 2 million shares outstanding and its current stock price is $64.20, then its market capitalization is $128.40 million (or 2 million x $64.20).

Market cap varies with a change in the price of a share. The higher the share price, the higher the market capitalization. The importance of this number lies in the fact that it tells investors about the desirability of a company. The higher the market cap for a given company, the less risky it is.

Listed companies are categorized into mega-caps, large-caps, mid-caps, and small-caps. There are smaller companies whose market caps fall into micro and nano categories. Let me briefly discuss the first four categories.

- Mega-cap stocks: These are publicly traded companies that have over $200 billion in market cap. Few companies have this size of market cap. Conspicuous examples of mega-cap stocks include Apple Inc., which reached a market cap of $2.08 trillion in March 2021 (Kolakowski, 2021).

- Large-cap stocks: A company with a market cap of from $10 billion to $200 billion is a large-cap stock. A good example is General Electric. Together with mega-cap stocks, large-cap stocks are popularly known as blue chip companies.

- Mid-cap stocks: Companies in this category have market caps ranging from $2 billion to $10 billion. Such companies tend to be more volatile than mega-cap and large-cap stocks. Several growth stocks have market caps in this range. One such company is Pinnacle West Capital Corporation, a holding company that supplies electricity based in Phoenix, Arizona.

- Small-cap stocks: These are companies that have from $500 million to $2 billion in market cap. This category is dominated by young companies that are riskier than mid-caps, large-caps, and mega-caps. However, they can deliver excellent capital growth to investors.

Company Management

Fundamental analysis cannot be complete without evaluating a target company's management team. There is no doubt that the quality of management influences the performance of a business. You can think of Apple when Steve Jobs ran it before being fired and when he returned.

Some retail investors often overlook the impact of management in their analysis of a stock. That's a big mistake. It is also a risky approach to invest in companies that rely on the reputation, skill, and talent of a single individual. Such a business could be vulnerable to the possibility of the person resigning or retiring and leaving the business in a predicament.

Those are some of the factors and metrics to consider when you study the fundamentals of a business. Using these fundamentals will enable you to select stocks to investigate further before investing in them.

Although fundamental analysis is useful in selecting stocks, it falls short in helping you time your entry to the market. This is the job better done by using an approach called technical analysis.

Technical Analysis

Technical analysis is an approach used to forecast future stock prices based on their current behavior. Technical analysts believe that the existing price of a stock reflects everything that's known about a company, including investor psychology and economic climate. By knowing the potential future price, traders and investors can time their entry into the market.

Stock prices move in waves where a buying wave is always followed by a selling wave or vice versa. In the old days, before the invention of sophisticated computers, traders and investors relied on a tape to read the behavior of a stock. A tape is a strip of paper that shows the transactions that took place in the stock market. Traders would manually transfer stock prices and other vital information onto graphs or charts for the purpose of easy analysis. In modern days, these tapes have been replaced by large electronic screens.

Today, investors and traders access various charts on trading platforms. Charts show trends and, thus, help analysts understand what a stock price may do in the near future. The most important function of a chart to a trader or investor is that it helps them time their entry or exit from a trade. Let me provide a short description of three important charts every trader and investor should be familiar with.

Types of Charts

History has a way of repeating itself. Stock prices also tend to repeat their past behavior. Traders and analysts find the past behaviors of stocks on charts. The most important charts include bar charts, line charts, and candlestick charts. All these charts technically convey similar information. It's the presentation that's different amongst them.

The Bar Chart

A bar chart shows a stock's price action in the form of thin, vertical bars. Each bar represents the opening, high, low, and closing (OHLC) prices over a given period of analysis, such as daily, hourly, or monthly. A single bar starts at the opening price and terminates at the high price level.

There are two short horizontal lines that start from the vertical bar. The short line on the left side of the bar represents the opening price, while the one on the right stands for the closing price. The difference between the high and low prices is called the trading range. The figure below illustrates what the bar chart looks like.

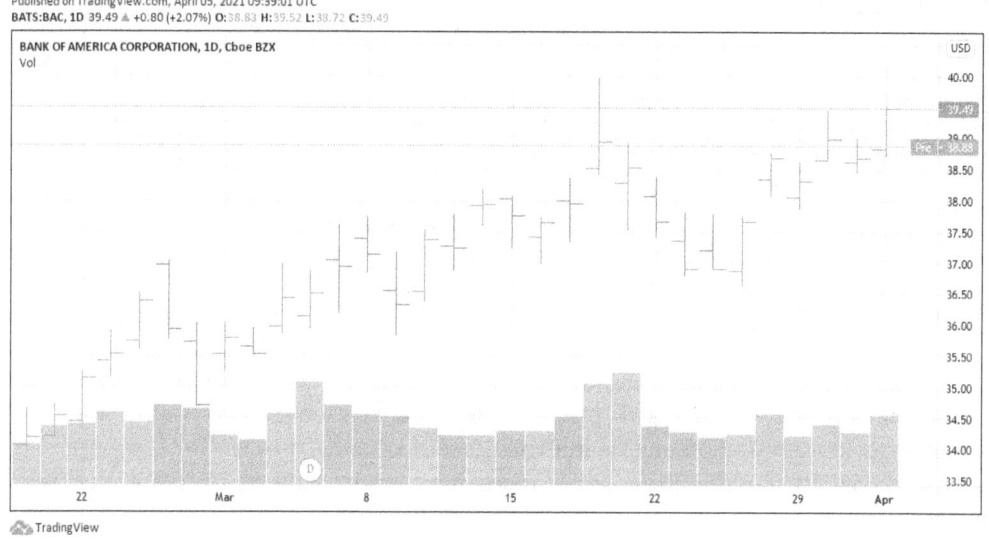

You'll notice that the chart has red and green vertical lines. The green vertical lines indicate that the closing price was higher than the opening price on the day. In contrast, the red-colored vertical bar shows that the stock closed at a lower price than its opening price.

The horizontal axis represents the frequency at which the chart is plotted. In the example chart above, the prices are tracked daily. The vertical bars at the bottom show the number of shares of the stock that were traded on the day. This number is often called the volume of shares and conveys important information when combined with price movements.

The Line Chart

A line chart results from plotting either the opening prices, closing prices, and highs or lows, joining them with a line. However, the closing prices are used more often, as in the chart shown below.

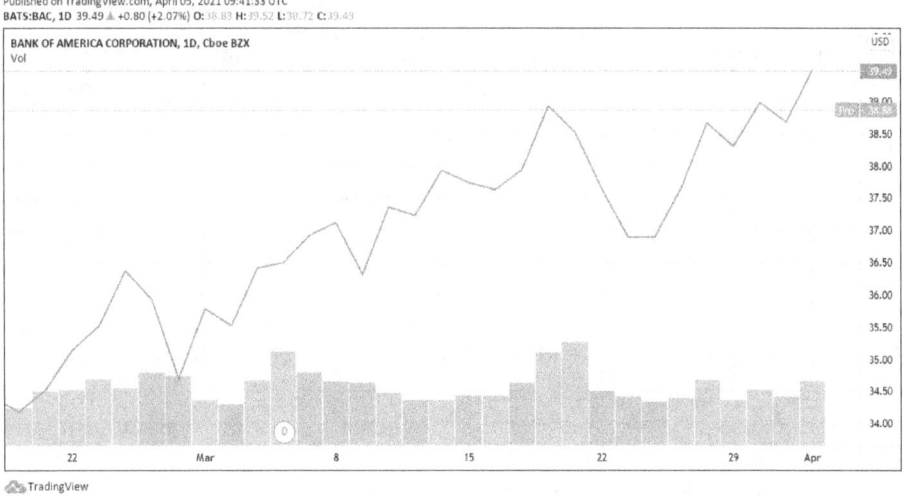

It is easier to analyze the price movements from the line graph. As you can see, the line chart also includes the volume of shares transacted.

The Candlestick Chart

A candlestick is similar to a bar chart in that it consists of a vertical bar showing the opening, high, low, and closing prices. However, the vertical bar of a candlestick has a thick part that's either shaded or unshaded, called the real body. The real body, when shaded, is colored in either red or green, as illustrated in the chart below.

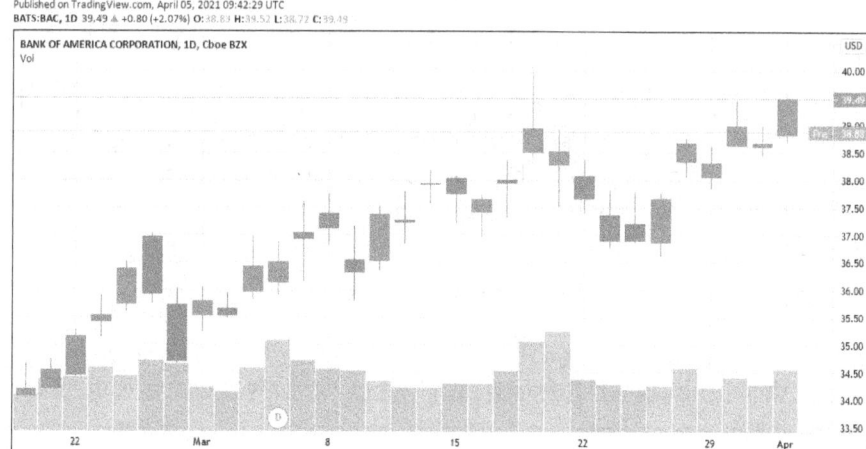

When the real body is red-shaded, the opening price is higher than the closing price. The green-shaded real body denotes that the opening price is lower than the closing price.

Technical Indicators Improve Decision-Making

Technical analysts use indicators to help them analyze stock prices on various charts. Indicators are tools you add to stock charts to assist in predicting the next behavior of a stock or stock market. They use price action, the volume of transactions, and time to reveal trends, support, and resistance levels.

There are several technical indicators available to assist you in decision-making. The most important thing is to know the purpose of each so that you can select the appropriate one for what you want to achieve. In general, indicators fall into two groups, those that standalone and others that are added to charts as overlays. The overlay types react with changing stock prices while the standalone indicators are added to their own charts, usually under the price chart.

Common Technical Indicators

There are certain indicators that almost every technical analyst should be familiar with. You can find most of these on trading platforms. These indicators are divided by function in the following way:

- Indicators used to find the support and resistance levels of a stock price action.
- Types that smooth a stock's price action.
- Indicators used to gauge the momentum of a stock's price movement.

Let's briefly discuss examples of each of the above functions.

Indicators Used to Smooth Price Action

Indicators that are used to smooth a stock's price action are plotted on a price chart. The easiest and quickest example to understand is the moving average. A moving average is a number that is continuously calculated as more data points become available. For example, for a 30-minute 20-period moving average, 20 consecutive data points are taken every 30 minutes and used to calculate the average. The process will repeat itself after every 30 minutes. In chart analysis, the moving average is plotted as trading time progresses.

There are several moving averages you can use on stock charts, such as a 50-simple moving average (SMA) and a 200-SMA. A 50-SMA means that the moving average results from including 50 consecutive data points in its calculation. When both the 50-SMA and 200-SMA are included in a chart, the 200-SMA will be smoother and take longer to turn. The figure below shows how the 50-SMA appears on a chart.

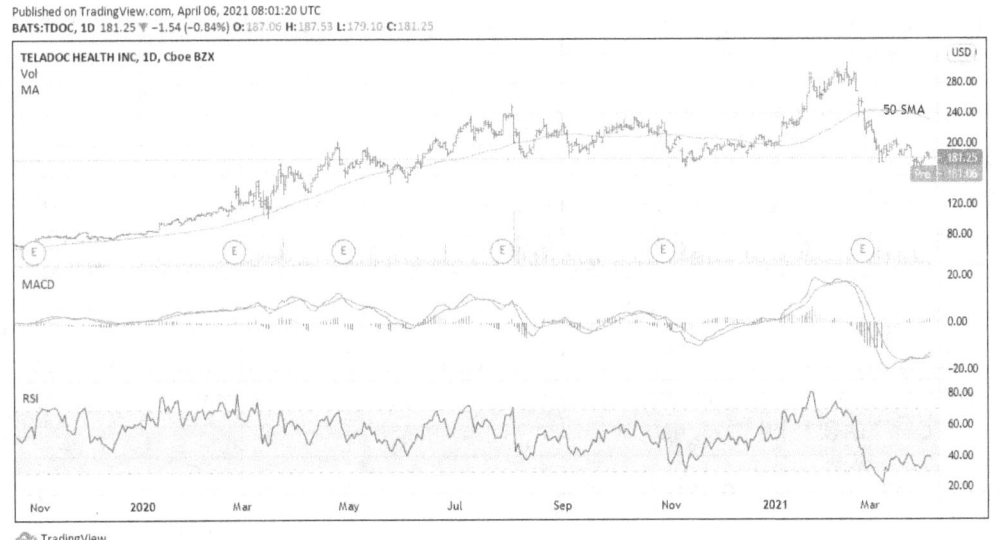

Momentum Indicators

Momentum indicators show the strength or weakness in a stock price. There are several such indicators, but we'll talk about only three here.

Relative Strength Indicator

A relative strength indicator (RSI) is a momentum indicator that allocates a stock price a value that lies between zero and 100. When the RSI falls below 30, the stock is considered oversold. This means that the stock has reached the lowest price because many traders and investors would have sold their shares. At this level, there is a strong chance that the stock price might bounce up.

When the RSI is above 70, a stock is overbought. This means that there are fewer investors and traders buying the stock, and the price is about to stop rallying. At this sort of RSI level, an investor or trader may sell or begin to sell the stock short. I'll explain in the next chapter what it means to short a stock.

Stochastic Oscillator

A stochastic oscillator is an indicator that consists of two oscillators called the fast %K and the slow %D. The latter is a 3-period moving average of the %K oscillator. Like the RSI, a stochastic oscillator assigns a stock price value between zero and 100 to indicate either an oversold or overbought situation. A value over 80 denotes that a stock is overbought, while a figure below 20 signifies a stock that is oversold. A stochastic oscillator is based on the theory that closing prices finish near a trading period's high in an uptrend market. Also, it considers that opening prices are closer to lows in a downtrending market.

Moving Average Convergence Divergence

A moving average convergence divergence (MACD) consists of two moving averages of a stock price. However, the moving averages are not the simple types but rather exponential moving averages (EMA). EMA is a moving average that puts more weight and importance on the most recent stock prices. By definition, MACD is a difference between a 12-period EMA and a 26-period EMA.

MACD can be either negative or positive depending on the relative sizes of the EMA's mentioned above. It is often plotted with a histogram that indicates the distance between a MACD and its signal line.

Support and Resistance Indicators

In chart analysis, there are prices that represent support and resistance levels. A support level is a stock price that seems to stop the stock from going further down. The other name for support is floor level. A support signals that demand for a stock is higher than supply. Often, this would happen when a stock is in an oversold condition.

In contrast, a resistance is a stock price that prevents further upward movement as it rallies. It is sometimes called a ceiling. At this point, the supply of a stock exceeds its demand.

A 100-SMA can act as a resistance or support. Depending on other indicators, when a moving average acts as a support for a price action, you may buy the charted stock. A moving average acting as a resistance may signal an opportunity to sell a long position or shorting a stock.

Chapter 3: Shorting a Stock—What It Means

A stock market goes up and down as trading time progresses. Most investors focus on only making money when a stock market goes up. This is logical when the market is bullish because most stocks follow suit. However, such investors stay away from taking positions when a stock market is in a bullish phase. Yet, there are stock market participants such as speculators who make money on both sides of a stock market. It is far riskier to invest in a stock when it is declining because you have to short it.

What Is to Short Sell a Stock?

Short selling a stock involves buying and selling shares you do not own. You head over to your broker and borrow a number of shares of a given stock. Your broker, if they have the shares, will lend you the shares. Then, you sell those shares at the prevailing market price. You do this transaction with the hope that the stock price will drop, allowing you to buy the shares you sold at a lower price and return them to your broker.

A closer look at short selling reveals that it works in an opposite way to the normal process where you buy first before selling. In short selling, you do the opposite in that you sell first and buy later. The strategy works for you only if you buy back the shares at a lower price than you borrowed them. It is how you make a profit before paying fees and commissions. Let me illustrate with concrete numbers how short selling works.

Suppose that you have been watching how a stock of a fictitious company called Advanced Micra Corporation (AMC) is performing. On a certain day, you notice that it is a good candidate to short when the price hits $40. You have done your homework and strongly believe the stock's price would decline to around $35. As a result, you decide to borrow 1,000 shares of the stock at $40, having ascertained that your broker can lend you the shares. This means the shares would have cost you $40,000.

Luckily, a few weeks later, the stock reaches a price of $34.50, which is close enough to your target price of $35. Not wanting to wait any longer, you decide to buy back the 1,000 shares at a price of $34.50 for a total sum of $34,500. You return the shares to your broker, and you make $5,500 ($40,000 - $34,500) before fees and commissions. That's how short selling works if things go your way.

However, it may happen that the price rises instead of declining after you short it. How would the picture look compared to the first scenario? Let's create a hypothetical scenario to see what would happen. Suppose AMC's stock price rises to $42.30 and you decide to cover your short. Covering a short position means that you buy back the borrowed shares of a stock. In this case, you'll pay $42,300 ($42.30 x 1,000) to buy back the shares. As a result, you'll lose $2,300 ($40,000 - $42,300) in the process.

It's clear that short selling can be risky, especially if you don't do your homework properly. There are many speculators and hedge funds who make money through this process. The big danger is that the price of a short stock can rise up to infinity. Thus, theoretically, there is no limit to how much a speculator can lose by shorting stocks. In contrast, investors who make money by taking long positions can only lose a maximum of their capital if the share declines to $0.

When you short stock, the buyer of your shares is eligible to receive any dividends declared while you're holding your short position. You don't have to worry about how you'll ensure the buyer receives their dividends. Your broker will handle the payment of the dividends. The issue of dividend payments is not a big one because a stock price normally declines by the dividend amount when it goes ex-dividend. You also don't have to pay any interest on the amount of borrowed shares because you use a margin account to short sell a stock. This makes sense since your broker does not lend you money. They get their share from the proceeds of the complete transaction.

Short Selling in the Right Market

There is a trading rule that savvy investors and traders keep in their minds all the time. The rule says that you should never trade against the market. In other words, when the market is bullish, they go long to make money on increasing prices, while they go short in a bearish market. This does not mean that you cannot go short in an uptrending market. You can, but the risk of losing capital is greatly multiplied. It is far easier to make money in shorting stock when the market is bearish. However, there is still a potential risk, such as a short squeeze, a topic we will discuss later in this chapter.

Knowing that short selling works better in a bear market suggests that your main job is to identify the start of such a market phase. A complete speculator has the ability to make money on both sides of the market. Analysis of the stock market or a share over a long period of time shows that the bear phase proceeds faster than the bullish stage. See the chart of the S&P below, which covers a period of five years.

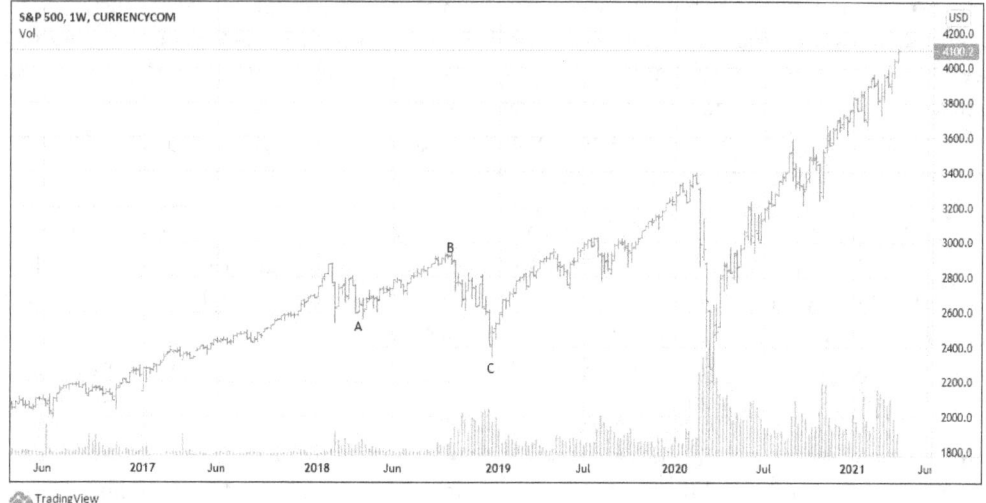

The bull phase of interest began at point A on March 19, 2018, and ended at B on September 17, 2018. This bull market took nearly six months to run its course. The succeeding bear phase began at B and ended at C on December 24, 2018. Thus, the bear market proceeded for just three months. So, the bear market, in this case, was two times faster than the preceding bull market. Looking closely at the chart confirms that the bear market seems to run faster than its corresponding bull market (mostly). There may be exceptions, but they are few.

Richard Demille Wyckoff, author of *How I Invest in Stocks and Bonds*, observed a similar phenomenon explained above and explained it in the 1930s as follows:

"Supply in a falling market rotates more rapidly than demand in a rising market. This is explained by the fact that there is seldom (if ever) sufficient buying power to lift all stocks at once in bull movements, whereas, in bear movements, fear, necessity, or both, eventually compel holders to liquidate all stocks without regard to value" (Section 8M, page 6 Wyckoff course).

Another important reason for this behavior of stocks and the market is that long positions attract investors more than short positions do.

The above suggests that an investor or trader must be adept at timing the start of the bear market. This would allow them to short the market early and exit before it is too late. Every speculator and investor interested in shorting the market or stocks must study stock market averages and indices such as the Dow Jones Industrial Average (DJIA), Nasdaq, and S&P 500. They are extremely important because they track some of the most liquid and well-established companies in the stock market. Instead of using one stock market performance metric, it may be a good idea for an investor to employ all the three market indicators mentioned above.

When all show strong signs that the market is becoming bearish, you'll know it would be the right time to consider shorting some stocks. What's next is to choose the right stocks to short.

How to Choose Stocks to Short

Investors and traders do not short just any stock. There are certain characteristics and stock behaviors to watch for before you short a stock. When the market is trending upwards, there are always stocks that outperform it. In other words, they rise faster than the whole market as measured by an index or average. This means that you can follow such stocks or an average that you create based on a few of such stocks to identify the end of the bull run. At that point, these stocks would have attracted a large following of both the public and institutional investors, such as mutual funds, banks, and pension funds.

Wyckoff noticed that "Bull markets unusually begin with advances in the leaders, that is, the seasoned, higher grade, and higher priced issues." He went on to say, "This is so because the big interests, who are best informed as to the prospects for approaching recovery, dominate these stocks and hence reflect their sentiments toward the market by their operations in the leaders."

This tells you that you should short stocks that decline faster than the market as a whole. The reason is that the market would soon follow these leading stocks, and you want that from happening while you are already in the game. This strategy also helps you avoid getting in late and be forced to close your short positions at losses.

What Short Interest Is

It is a big advantage to a trader to know if a certain stock is a target of short sellers. How would you know if you wanted to? The way to know if a stock is being sold short is to look at short interest. To determine short interest, you divide the number of shorted shares by the number of shares outstanding. The best way to express short interest is in percentages because it is often a small number. If a stock has been short 250,000 shares out of a total of 1.5 million shares outstanding, it has a short interest of 16.67% (250,000/1.5 million x 100). Armed with the short interest of a given stock, you'll quickly know what the prevailing market sentiment is on the stock. In other words, you'll know whether the market is bullish or bearish on the particular stock.

The second way to present short interest is by a metric called the days-to-cover ratio. This tells you how long it would take for short sellers to exit their position and avoid a short squeeze. You obtain this ratio by dividing the number of shorted stocks by the average daily trading volume. For example, on November 30, 2020, Otonomy, Inc., a company founded by Dr. Jay Lichter to assist patients with hearing disorders, was shorted 817,050 shares, and its average daily trading volume was 203,059. So, its short interest was a days-to-cover ratio of 4.024. It would have taken short sellers about five days to close their positions in time.

Numerous days-to-cover denotes that traders are more bearish on the stock. However, this may open a chance for a big short squeeze if the trades are wrong. A short squeeze is a huge leap in a stock's price as a result of investor buying that's supported by short sellers closing their positions to minimize their losses. Vulnerable stocks often have smaller floats and high short interest.

Stock exchanges often report short interest at the end of every month. However, the Nasdaq reports it twice a month, first in the middle and the second at the end of the month. As you track short interest, you may observe a large change (an increase or decrease) from one month to the next. That is an indication the market sentiment might be changing. For example, a stock's short interest may increase from 15% to 30%. This means that the number of speculators shorting the stock has doubled. You may want to investigate the deeper reason for the sentiment.

It is important to track short interest on a stock to notice when market sentiment is changing. This helps you overcome the challenge of delayed reporting of short interest. A month is too long for the stock market because many things can change during that period. By the time you establish a certain market sentiment on a stock, it might be too late to act. However, studying short interest over a long period of time arms you with a sixth sense, especially when combined with other indicators.

Besides short interest, investors and traders may use a put/call ratio to figure out market sentiment. A put/call ratio utilizes the options market for calculations. Share options are contracts that give the bearer the right to buy or sell a certain amount of shares by a certain date without obligation. A put option is a bet used by a bearish investor, while a call option is a bullish bet. When the put/call ratio of a share changes, market sentiment shifts from bullish to bearish or vice versa.

Like with all investment and trading tools, short interest should not be used singly to make investing decisions. Use other tools to confirm what short interest is telling you.

Chapter 4: Is the Stock Market Rigged?

Bankrate recently undertook a survey among 2,525 American adults to gauge their investing habits. Among the questions included in the survey, Bankrate wanted to know if participants thought the stock market was rigged. Results showed that 48% of the surveyed people felt that the stock market is rigged against retail investors. However, 13% of the participants disagreed, and only 5% of these strongly disagreed that the stock market is manipulated against the small investor. A typical person likely to believe the stock market is rigged tends to be a male, below age 40, a college graduate, earns over $50,000, and they are an investor.

The big question that I have for you is this: "Do you believe that the stock market is rigged against any retail investor?" Whether you believe it or not, we have to go to the facts to settle the answer to the question. You'll find two cases in this chapter that prove beyond doubt that there are market participants who do not play a fair game. You may remember that the financial market connects savers with investors. Many times, as we have already shown in Chapter 1, there is a middleman connecting the two parties. It is these financial intermediaries that can have so much power as to influence the movement of the markets, especially if they invest in the same securities.

When you see the phrase "institutional investors," you should know that we are referring to big financial intermediaries such as investment banks and pension funds. These stock market participants tend to have more power to shift the prices of securities compared to individual investors. Advanced Micro Devices, Inc. (AMD) is a company whose stock is listed on the Nasdaq. At this writing, institutional investors hold 71.22% of the traded shares. This means that the balance is in the hands of insiders and retail investors. Who would say has a better chance of shifting the stock price of AMD? Obviously, it is the institutional investors. If you consider that some of these have to report their holdings to the SEC, you cannot help but recognize that these market participants can influence each other to invest or divest from a stock. Let's return to our subject of market manipulation.

The SEC defines market manipulation as anything done to interfere with the operation of the law of supply and demand of a security. Remember that the law of supply determines the prices of securities. Often, culprits of this unlawful practice intend to deceive individual investors by artificially driving a security's price either upward or downward.

There are numerous reasons why market manipulation is bad, including the following.

- It may push investors out of the market and, in turn, this could result in ineffective markets.
- It defeats the objective of running a fair, honest, and orderly market.

- It can either inflate or deflate prices of securities and thus nullify the objective judgment of buyers and sellers of a security.
- It could damage the reputation of a marketplace and potentially result in failure by businesses to raise money to develop the country's economy.

Manipulators could be anyone and can include insiders, brokers, or large stock market participants such as investment bankers. Insiders can manipulate securities through deceptive accounting and reporting false information. Because market manipulators practice unlawful activities, we have to go behind the scenes to understand how they work.

We are fortunate because some of the market manipulations could be detected on the price action of a security. However, in some cases, the manipulated activities can be hidden from plain view, even on the price of a security.

Prices of securities often reflect the actions of the major market participants. This means that the performance of a stock reflects the methods and character of investors with large holdings in it. We must always keep in mind that the stock market is nothing but an agglomeration of the minds of market participants. The subject of market manipulation has been there even before the formation of the SEC. Sophisticated traders such as Richard Wyckoff studied and understood the operations of market manipulators operating behind the scenes.

Wyckoff believed that "Most of the important moves in the market are prepared, executed, and conclude." It is partly this observation that enabled Wyckoff to develop techniques to profit from the operations of stock manipulators. The duration of a stock manipulation campaign could take a day, a week, a month, or several months. For that reason, a stock price manipulator wouldn't buy numerous shares at once. They have to run a campaign in which they buy the shares they wanted over a certain period and in ways that hide their activity. In other words, market manipulators try to run a stealth operation to avoid being caught.

There are people who think that there is no such a thing as market or stock manipulation, as the earlier referenced Bankrate's survey shows. Some believe that with the presence of the SEC, manipulation would be a thing of the past. That's far from reality. The one thing that has changed is the method of manipulation. The intentions to rig stock prices are still there. Let's look at one case reported by the SEC in 2014.

Guilty as Charged for Market Manipulation

The SEC charged Athena Capital Research LLC. and released their findings on October 16, 2014. Athena, at the time, was a high-frequency trading firm operating from New York City. According to the SEC findings, Athena used complex algorithms to manipulate the closing prices of thousands of stocks on the Nasdaq for a period of about six months.

Athena's trading strategy involved buying or selling thousands of shares two seconds before the Nasdaq closed at 4:00 p.m. Their idea was to either push the closing prices of affected stocks either up or down, but always to their advantage. The program used to execute this strategy went by the name 'gravy.' By manipulating prices, Athena was able to make reliable profits from their risky operations.

According to the SEC, Athena was a small firm but dominated the stock market in the closing seconds of trading. For each stock they targeted, Athena traded in over 70% of the available volume in the last few seconds before the stock market closed. Athena did this sort of trading nearly every day by targeting the order imbalances in stocks as the stock market approached its closing time.

An order imbalance is a situation that results when there is an excess of buy or sell orders for a given stock. It can make it difficult to match buy and sell orders. An order imbalance can drive the price of a security either up or down and result in high volatility. To prevent this unwanted situation, the Nasdaq runs a closing auction to fill all on-close orders at prices close to the security's price in the order book (also called a continuous book). Part of the process involves sending out imbalance messages, and the first one reaches the market at 3:50 p.m.

Athena's trading strategy on imbalance messages worked like this: As soon as the Nasdaq issued its first imbalance message, Athena placed an imbalance only on close order to fill the imbalance. Only when there is an imbalance does the Nasdaq fill these orders. Thereafter, Athena would buy or sell the affected security on the order book. For example, if the order imbalance was to buy, Athena would place a sell order. They timed this activity with precision so that they held no positions by the time the Nasdaq closed. Let me illustrate the mechanics of Athena's money-making trading strategy.

You already know that when demand for a stock exceeds its supply, its price will rise. So, when an imbalance message shows that there's a need to buy, market makers expect the stock's closing price to rise since buying would drive the price up. In contrast, a selling imbalance message implies that the closing price would be lower than the existing price when the stock market closed.

Athena used this knowledge to craft a trading strategy that ensured that they earned money on imbalance messages. If the imbalance message was to buy 20,000 shares of a given stock, Athena placed a sell imbalance only order for 20,000 shares of the stock.

Thereafter, this high-frequency trading firm would try to buy 20,000 shares of the affected stock in the last 10 minutes before the stock market closed.

Conversely, if a sell imbalance message was for 20,000 shares, Athena placed a buy order for the same number of shares. Following this, they would accumulate short positions on 20,000 shares of the involved stock during the last 10 minutes before the market closure. Athena made sure that they exited their positions at the close of the market, knowing that the order would be filled at a better price than the average they paid to accumulate the shares. I'll illustrate this with one of the campaigns Athena ran.

The accumulation of shares that Athena carried out after the first imbalance message was called 'meat.' The name this company gave to the last two seconds trading method was termed 'gravy.' Here is how one manager is said to have described Athena's trading strategy: "We have a desired accumulation pattern which includes grabbing stock at the beginning, a period of 'average price' accumulation, and crescendo at the end." Using its sophisticated algorithm and quantitative analyses, Athena was able to place imbalance only orders before 3:50 p.m., a strategy they called 'collars.'

A good example of how Athena's strategy worked involved eBay's stock on November 25, 2009. Here's how the campaign panned out.

- Athena placed collars orders prior to 3:50 p.m.

- Nasdaq issued its first imbalance message at 3:50:00 p.m. The message showed a buy imbalance of 224,638 shares of eBay, and this stock traded at $23.55 at the time.

- At 3:50:00.578, Athena placed a sell imbalance only order for all the 224,638 shares of eBay at $0.01. This means that the order would be executed at the trading price plus $0.01. At the same time, Athena placed an order to buy 85,000 shares of eBay at $23.56 to kick-start their accumulation campaign. Almost instantly, 16,000 of those shares Athena ordered were filled.

- Next, Athena placed buy orders of between 100 and 5,800 shares of eBay and managed to buy 64,000 shares more between 3:50:07.004 and 3:59:58.112. After this, gravy kicked in milliseconds prior to 3;59:58 p.m. when the national best offer for eBay was $23.58. It placed six buy orders of volumes ranging from 5,600 to 33,600 shares at six different times. They placed the last order at 3:59:59.950.

    They secured 112,000 eBay shares at an average price of $23.594. This volume made up over 71% of eBay's entire market's volume in the final two seconds of trading. At 3:59:58.510, the national best offer price for eBay stock had moved to $23.59, and finally, at 3:59:59.963, it reached $23.60.

The Nasdaq ran its closing auction at 4:00:03.348, and Athena's sell imbalance only order was filled. However, not all of the order was filled because the actual amount sold was 223,979 for $23.61 a share, which was $0.03 higher than the best eBay's price before gravy came in.

The SEC considered this case the first involving a high-frequency trading firm. You have to wonder whether Athena was the only such company doing this kind of thing. There is no doubt that from the above example that high-frequency trading firms have an unfair advantage over individual investors. Is that what a free market means? I'll leave you with that question to ponder on it a bit.

There is no doubt from the case above that the people who suffer the most are the individual investors and ordinary citizens. Mutual funds depend on the closing prices of securities to adjust their investment portfolios. How can their strategies work for their investors if they are basing their decisions on manipulated data?

Market manipulation is not a phenomenon that began in our modern times. It has probably existed since the inception of the stock market. Richard Wyckoff explained how those in the know manipulated stock prices in some of his writings in the 1930s and earlier. I would like to share with you how back then, traders like Wyckoff spotted the operations of manipulators.

Wyckoff's Operation of the Composite Operator

Wyckoff named the combined forces that drove prices of stocks the composite operator. He believed there were forces behind the scenes that planned stock prices and caused them to move in their favor. However, there was a method behind their operations so that they could not be detected. What follows is a shortened version of the mechanism that the composite operator used to attain their trading objective. The numbers I'll use are arbitrary to illustrate a point.

Suppose a certain stock currently trades between $30 and $35 per share. The composite operator wants to accumulate 50,000 shares within that price range. Upon attaining this objective, they want to drive the price of the stock upward to a given target, such as $60, in the following few weeks or months.

They first place a buy order for a certain number of shares at a price near $30. Their aim is to pull the stock price closer to $30 a share. Then, they sell a large number of shares at a price closer to $30 and induce others to sell their long positions or short sell. A long position means that you buy and hold shares in anticipation of selling them at a higher price for profit. Short selling involves borrowing shares from a broker, selling them immediately, and later when the price is lower, buy and return them to the broker. We'll talk about this concept in more detail in Chapter 5.

If the composite operator sells 10,000 shares, they may buy 20,000 shares and have a net accumulation of 10,000 shares. As long as the stock prices remain low, others are more likely to avoid buying the stock. This gives the composite operator an opportunity to keep buying until they have their target number of shares. Some of the techniques the composite operator uses include distributing bearish news to persuade weaker investors to sell their shares due to fear.

The aim of the first stage of the composite operator's campaign is to accumulate stocks at their target prices. This is synonymous with the accumulation strategy that Athena used to profit from closing prices of stocks, as discussed earlier. Once the first stage is complete, they are ready for the next phase, called markup. That's the period when the price of a stock rallies. A study of a stock's price action and volume of transactions will show you that there are people who buy as a stock's price trends upwards. The reason behind this behavior is mostly greed. The chart below shows a trading range bounded by a combination of a support and a resistance. Accumulation of shares in the chart below occurs between points A and B. You can see that as soon as accumulation is complete, the price shoots up.

Note that I am not saying someone was manipulating the stock represented in this chart. I am using it to illustrate a point. You can check many other stocks' price actions, and you're likely to find patterns like this. What you are seeing is human psychology at play. It is this human element that manipulators take advantage of.

I should mention that the markup stage during the composite operator's campaign often coincides with some bullish news. The latter may come from various sources such as analysts, a company, or a hedge fund.

I would like to offer a second case of manipulation of stocks captured in the SEC files. The case did not involve high-frequency trading or big stock market players. It goes to show that there may be many manipulation activities in the stock market going unnoticed.

The SEC Charges an Actress for Her Role in Stock Manipulation

Actress Kamilla Bjorlin once played Countess Elan in the movie "The Princess Diaries 2: Royal Engagement." While pursuing her Hollywood career, Bjorlin was charged by the SEC for secretly paying writers to pump up stock prices of certain companies. Bjorlin ran Lidingo Holdings, a company formed in 2011 as a Nevada limited liability firm; it was dissolved in 2014. Lidingo's business was to help publicly traded companies with stock promotion activities. She mostly promoted her clients via investment articles posted on websites such as Seeking Alpha.

The SEC alleged that Bjorlin, supported by others, was paid by stock issuers for her services. From September 2011 to March 2014, Lidingo worked with 14 different writers, 11 publicly traded companies, and at least 400 publications. When Bjorlin finished her stock promotion work, stock issuers paid her company, and in turn, she paid the writers who penned blog articles that were published on certain websites. In one case, Lidingo is alleged to have helped Galena Biopharma, a small pharmaceutical company, shoot up its stock price by 925%.

Judgment on the Bjorlin case with the SEC was delivered by the Honorable Ricardo S. Martinez at the United States District Court, Western District of Washington at Seattle on January 8, 2020. It really can take that long for the law to take its course. In giving his judgment, Honorable Martinez decided that:

> Bjorlin is permanently restrained and enjoined from violating Section 17(a) of the Securities Act of 1933 ("Securities Act"), 15 U.S.C. § 77q(a), in the offer or sale of any security by the use of any means or instruments of transportation or

communication in interstate commerce or by use of the mails, directly or indirectly: (i) to employ any device, scheme, or artifice to defraud; (ii) to obtain money or property by means of any untrue statement of a material fact or any omission of a material fact necessary in order to make the statements made, in light of the circumstances under which they were made, not misleading; or (iii) to engage in any transaction, practice, or course of business which operates or would operate as a fraud or deceit upon the purchaser.

Image by Anna Varsányi from Pixabay

Bjorlin's charges included a disgorgement of $437,611, prejudgment interest of $107,601, and a fine of $160,000 for her role in the scheme. That brings the total to $705,212.

The two cases covered above provide enough evidence to conclude that market manipulation cannot be ruled out completely. Yes, it is outlawed, but it does happen. This does not mean that every participant on the stock market practices market manipulation and underhanded activities like insider trading. The stock market itself might not be rigged, but there are probably securities that are being manipulated.

It is really upon an individual investor to protect themselves from stock manipulators. It is true that such a task won't be easy. However, if not done, by the time manipulators are found, it may be too late for an individual investor. One great way of protecting yourself as an individual investor is by acquiring investment competency and stop relying on people you are not sure what their motives are. Also, you'll be able to make most, if not all, of your investment decisions without asking for someone's opinion.

Chapter 5: Major Short Squeezes Every Trader Should Know About

Short squeezes have been part of the stock market for years. The recent GameStop short squeeze is unique because of the type of investors who were heavily involved in it. Tesla was also the subject of a short squeeze in 2020. However, the GameStop short squeeze is likely to change the way the stock market runs. It is a good idea to go back in time and learn how short squeezes took place in the past. The information we glean may be valuable in protecting ourselves and our money from ruthless large stock market participants. Also, we'll establish the real way that the stock market actually works—not what the theory says.

The Piggly Wiggly® Short Squeeze

Piggly Wiggly® was a chain of self-service retail stores known in modern times as supermarkets, founded in 1919. It was listed on the New York Stock Exchange (NYSE) in 1922. The listing set the stage for one of a stock market history of short squeezes in the last 100 years. Piggly Wiggly® stores was the brainchild of a Memphis native named Clarence Saunders. The short squeeze we'll discuss involved Saunders and Wall Street operators eager to enrich themselves without having accurate facts of the situation.

A closer look at what happens during a short squeeze shall convince you that it is a high-stakes gambling game between the bulls and the bears. The bulls buy more and more of a stock that the bears short in high numbers. In the days of Piggly Wiggly® stores, short sellers knew little about the identities of the buyer(s) of their borrowed stock as well as the owner(s) of the original stock. The situation is still the same in our modern days. It is quite possible that the buyer and lender of the stocks is the same stock market participant. So, a short seller operates in the dark unless they are involved in deliberate market manipulation.

Short sellers not only orchestrate a spree of short selling, they often spread rumors about how bad the targeted company is. This is to be expected because we tend to rationalize our actions even if they are wrong. Upon hearing this news, the uninformed public become fearful and begin to offload their holdings. As this happens, the price of the stock declines and keeps doing so unless someone begins to buy the stock. Not everyone may see what short sellers perceive about the affected company. There may be investors who see potential in the business and argue that the company is more valuable than the short sellers estimate. As a result, they may begin to buy the stock, and in so doing, bring the stock price decline to a halt. Doing so in a heavily shorted stock could result in a short squeeze. All that's necessary is to buy as much of the floating supply of stock as possible. Furthermore, the bull may also buy as much of the company's privately held shares as possible. Let's return to the story of Piggly Wiggly®.

After Piggly Wiggly® was founded, it grew by leaps and bounds, and in 1922 it boasted 1,200 stores. Over half of the stores (650) belonged to Saunders, while the balance were franchisees. It is this growth and the desire to expand that led Saunders to list the company on the NYSE. It took only six months for Piggly Wiggly® to become one of the regular dividend-paying companies on the stock market. However, things were to turn from good to bad in November 1922. Several franchisees of Piggly Wiggly® in New York, New Jersey, and Connecticut failed, and creditors swiftly moved to recoup their monies through receivership.

When a gang of stock market operators saw these developments, they smelled an opportunity to make money through shorting Piggly Wiggly®. It is easier to mount a short on a listed company when it is going through rough times. You can spread rumors far easier, and the public is likely to believe you even if the news may not be factual. Most ordinary people barely take the time to verify what they hear from the rumor mill or media, partly because they do not trust themselves. Furthermore, the public is usually not well-informed about the way a business truly works, as well as how a stock market works.

The bears who saw Piggly Wiggly® as a good candidate for shorting did not waste time in selling it short. As they expected, the stock soon yielded to the selling pressure, and its price declined from a year high of about $50 to $40 a share. It must have been painful for Saunders as he watched, nearly helplessly, as his company's stock plummeted. After thinking the matter over, Saunders decided that he should do something, and soon.

He resolved that he was going to operate a buying campaign to support the stock of Piggly Wiggly® and beat Wall Street at their game. To give the investing public confidence in his company, he announced his intentions in the media. At the time Saunders did this, he had never owned stock of a company listed on the NYSE. It follows that Saunders knew little about a short squeeze and let alone how to execute it. However, his actions seemed like he knew how to cause short sellers unprecedented psychological pain. From the onlooker, Saunders was protecting his investment and the investments of his company's stockholders.

Saunders did not have the funds to consummate the campaign. So, he borrowed $10 million from bankers in Memphis, Nashville, New Orleans, Chattanooga, and St. Louis and combined it with his own funds. The campaign was so big it would have been nearly impossible for one person to carry it through successfully. Saunders recruited a group of brokers to assist him. Among these brokers, he included Jesse L. Livermore, one of a few top traders at the time, whom he chose to lead the execution of the campaign.

The campaign got off to a flying start in that Saunders bought 33,000 shares of Piggly Wiggly® on its first day. By the end of the first week, the number had leaped to 105,000 shares, which represented over 50% of 200,000 shares of Piggly Wiggly® outstanding. When January 23rd arrived, Saunders had managed to drive up the stock price to over $60. Reports started to come from the Chicago Stock Exchange (where the stock was also traded) that short sellers in Piggly Wiggly® were short squeezed. However, NYSE comforted the short sellers and the public that Piggly Wiggly® still had ample float.

Encouraged by the news from Chicago, Saunders wrote and published a newspaper advertisement offering 50,000 shares at $55 a share. This was clearly a good offer relative to the existing trading price of the stock. Another advertisement followed, still keeping the offer at $55 per share. The second advertisement appeared while Piggly Wiggly® was trading at $70 a share on the NYSE. I wonder who was advising Saunders on this campaign. Whoever it was must have advised Saunders that if the shares returned to the short sellers, the short squeeze would be broken.

Cleverly, Saunders offered the shares he sold on a three-month installment plan. The buyer had to pay down $25 and the remainder in three installments to be paid on June 1st, September 1st, and December 1st. This arrangement was ingenious because Saunders had to keep the share certificates with him until the buyer paid for all the shares. By that time, Saunders knew that the short sellers would have suffered.

By March 19th, Saunders had nearly all the Piggly Wiggly® shares that were available for trading. Clearly, the short squeeze was on. Saunders wanted Livermore to spring the trap and send the short sellers scrambling to cover their positions. However, Livermore had exited the campaign days previously, possibly fearing being implicated if the market were to suffer due to Saunder's campaign. As a result, Saunders released the news of the trap himself on March 20th.

On that day, Piggly Wiggly® stock opened at $75.50, a rise of $5.50 compared to the previous day's closing price. The news of the trap surfaced an hour after the opening of the stock exchange. In essence, the news said that Saunders wanted short sellers to return the stock they borrowed. The bears had nowhere else to find the shares but from Saunders himself. Unsurprisingly, the stock price of Piggly Wiggly® jumped to $90, then $100, and then $110. One Piggly Wiggly® investor who owned 1,100 shares sold their holdings at $105 a share and pocketed over $70,000 in profit.

By the afternoon, the Piggly Wiggly® share price had gone up to $124, the highest it ever went since listing. At that time, news came to the exchange floor that governors of the NYSE were meeting to consider suspending the stock and increasing the deadline for the short sellers to deliver their borrowed shares. It didn't take long for the Piggly Wiggly® stock price to decline to $82 due to the negative news.

After the Governing Committee of the Exchange met, they announced a trading suspension on the Piggly Wiggly® stock and extended the delivery deadline for the short sellers. No one gave an immediate official reason for the decisions. It's clear, based on the facts on hand, that the exchange wanted to protect the short sellers. Why did they do this? You'll notice as we proceed that this behavior wasn't the last. It seems the big boys of Wall Street aren't supposed to suffer major losses. Somehow something happens that releases the squeeze on these market participants. However, there are thousands of retail investors who lose their savings, and no one seems to care. At any rate, Piggly Wiggly® was permanently removed from the trading list, and Saunders was left to deal with a huge debt to his bankers.

A short squeeze did not first happen to Piggly Wiggly®, and it did not end with Saunders' company. There have been other short squeezes, including in the 21st century. We'll look at two more before we begin a thorough investigation into the GameStop short squeeze.

The Volkswagen Short Squeeze

The buildup to the Volkswagen short squeeze took years to materialize. Clearly, the events and processes that took place were not initially calculated to lead to a short squeeze. As is often the case, the business strategy and operations of a company set up a squeeze because short sellers look for news that they can use to their advantage. The key player in the Volkswagen squeeze was Porsche.

Let's start the story in 1931 when Ferdinand Porsche founded a business firm to serve the automotive sector in Germany. One of his standout projects was the design of the Volkswagen Beetle in 1934. Ferdinand Porsche went on to found Porsche AG, a carmaker, in 1948. The Porsche family controlled the business for over the next 50 years.

Over time, Porsche outsourced some of its manufacturing tasks to Volkswagen. That's not where the relationship between Volkswagen and Porsche ended. Ferdinand Piech, Ferdinand Porsche's grandson, joined the Volkswagen Group in 1993 as chief executive. Piech had spent the previous 30 years at Audi. When he took over Volkswagen, it had just recorded a $1.1 billion loss, but he returned the company back to profitability before his retirement and became chairman in 2002. While employed by Volkswagen, Piech and his family maintained a 50% stake in Porsche.

Wendelin Wiedeking, who had been a former Volkswagen board member, was then running Porsche and desired to take over Volkswagen. Two reasons were behind Wiedeking's intention. He and Porsche, the company, wanted to secure access to Volkswagen's manufacturing knowledge and expertise and also to block off any hostile takeover. Piech favored the merge of the two German carmakers because he knew he would still remain in control of the overall business.

It did not come as a surprise when, in 2005, Porsche announced that they had 20% voting (ordinary) shares rights in Volkswagen. By 2007, Porsche had raised their stake in Volkswagen to over 30%, a situation that mandated it to make a takeover offer. However, the attempt fell on deaf ears and failed. Porsche were not to be denied, though. The European Court of Justice gave them hope when it overturned the Volkswagen Act. This law had required anyone interested in taking over Volkswagen to own 80% of voting shares. It had been set up to prevent any hostile takeover of Volkswagen.

A 2007 Reuters article reported that Porsche said the failed bid meant that they would not have had to make more mandatory takeover attempts if they raised their stake in Volkswagen. As such, they had the flexibility to protect any attempt to take over Volkswagen by private equity businesses or hedge funds. It is apparent that Porsche wanted to prevent any other business from attempting to take Volkswagen from them. The best way Porsche could block other companies from buying Volkswagen was to buy more voting shares.

Wiedeking received a boost to pursue his intention when, in March 2008, Porsche's supervisory board approved the company's intention to increase their stake in Volkswagen to 50%. On September 16, 2008, Porsche raised its shareholding in Volkswagen to 35%.

At the time in Germany, nearly 30 companies on the Dax-100 had ordinary and preference shares on offer. Owners of preference shares don't have voting rights but receive fixed dividends. Volkswagen's preference shares traded way lower than its ordinaries. Volkswagen's ordinary shares had begun a gradual rise in price from about the time when Porsche began buying them. Preference shares were also rising. The ratio of the price of the preference to ordinary shares peaked at around 75% or so.

In around 2007, Volkswagen's preference shares began to rise slower than the ordinaries. Seeing this divergence, some of the investors began to short Volkswagen. In other words, they anticipated the ordinary shares in Volkswagen to begin to decline sooner. However, the ratio of preference shares to ordinaries began a steep decline. This suggests that the price of ordinary shares kept rising.

The truth was about to surface when in October 2008, equity markets tumbled in the wake of the folding of the Lehman Brothers. In contrast, Volkswagen's ordinary shares were rallying. By October 16th, Volkswagen's ordinary shares were trading at close to €400, which is €467.37 (Inflation Tool, n.d.) in today's money or $564.11 (XE Business, 2021) a share. This was astonishing considering the situation the equity market was in.

On October 26, 2008, Porsche issued a press release in Stuttgart. In it, they mentioned that Porsche Automobil Holding SE decided to disclose its shareholding due to what they called "dramatic distortions on the financial markets." Porsche revealed that they held 42.6% of Volkswagen's ordinary shares plus 31.5% in cash-settled options to hedge against Volkswagen's stock price risks. As such, Porsche held a total of 74.1% in Volkswagen. This situation doesn't differ much from the Piggly Wiggly® one when Saunders announced that he wanted his shares the short sellers borrowed from him.

Vitally, Porsche mentioned that they made the announcement because it had become clear that there were far more short positions on the Volkswagen stock than was expected. The press release went on to warn, "The disclosure should give so-called short sellers—meaning financial institutions which have betted or are still betting on a falling price in Volkswagen—the opportunity to settle their relevant positions without rush and without facing major risks."

The news shocked, terrified, and unsettled the short sellers. It was nearly impossible for every short seller to close their position. The following Monday, Volkswagen's ordinary shares opened at €348, meaning that it was 68% above the previous Friday's closing price. By the time the market closed, the shares had risen 149% from the day's opening price to €517. On Tuesday, the Volkswagen ordinary shares jumped to as high as €999, making the automaker the largest company in the world for a day based on its market cap. In the process, it leapfrogged the likes of Exxon Mobil, Petro China, and Microsoft.

Unlike Clarence Saunders, Porsche realized that their actions caused financial damage and generously provided the short sellers with extra liquidity of 5% so that the shorts could free themselves from the short squeeze. Following this, the Volkswagen shares dropped 50% to €497 by Friday of that week. The squeeze cost hedge funds a €20 billion loss. Wiedeking and Holger Harter (Porsche's CFO) were found not guilty of market manipulation charges in 2016. About 19 hedge funds, such as Greenlight Capital, were unsuccessful in their €1.2 billion civil claim against Porsche because the German Federal Court of Justice dismissed the case.

The Tesla Short Squeeze

Photo by Li Xiang on Unsplash

One of the United States stocks that has endured a high short interest is Tesla, the electric automaker. Igor Dusaniwsky, managing director of S3 Partners, a financial analysis firm, called the Tesla short "by far the longest unprofitable short I've ever seen" (Institutional investor/the longest). Some of the bears who had shorted Tesla such as Mark Spiegel, founder of Stanphyl Capital Partners, a small hedge fund, believed that individual investors were gobbling up Tesla's shares through apps such as Robinhood.

Spiegel thought that COVID-19-induced staying at home was partly to blame for the gambling mentality of some institutional investors. The chart below shows the number of shorted Tesla shares from February 2019 to March 2021.

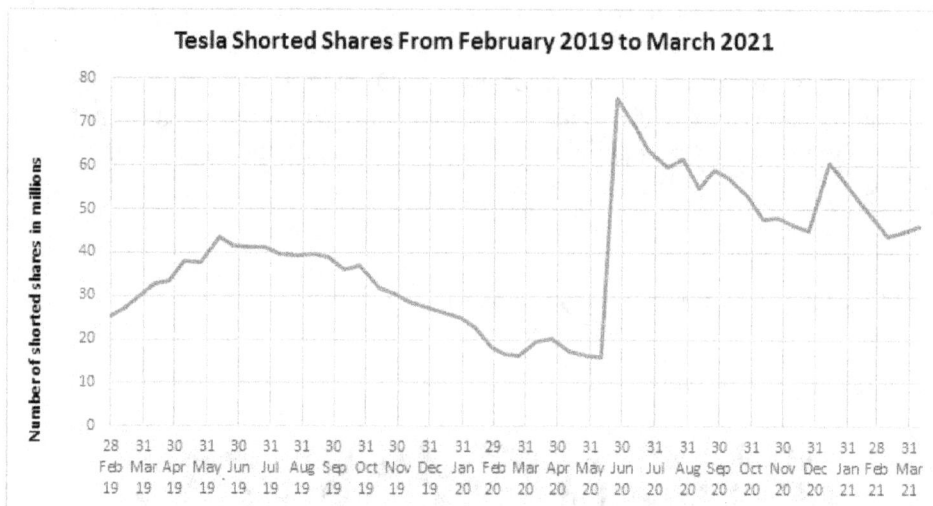

The number of shorts skyrocketed from 16 million in June 2020 to nearly 76 million shares. That's an increase of 375% in the number of shorted shares. That's an astounding increase. There is no doubt that the bears sensed an opportunity to score big with a possible drop in Tesla's stock price. However, the short sellers were running the risk of being squeezed out at losses.

Following its quarter three of 2019 results, Tesla's stock price leaped from $50.44 to a peak of about $183 per share on February 19, 2020. This represents a price rise of just under 263%. See the chart below for the price increase.

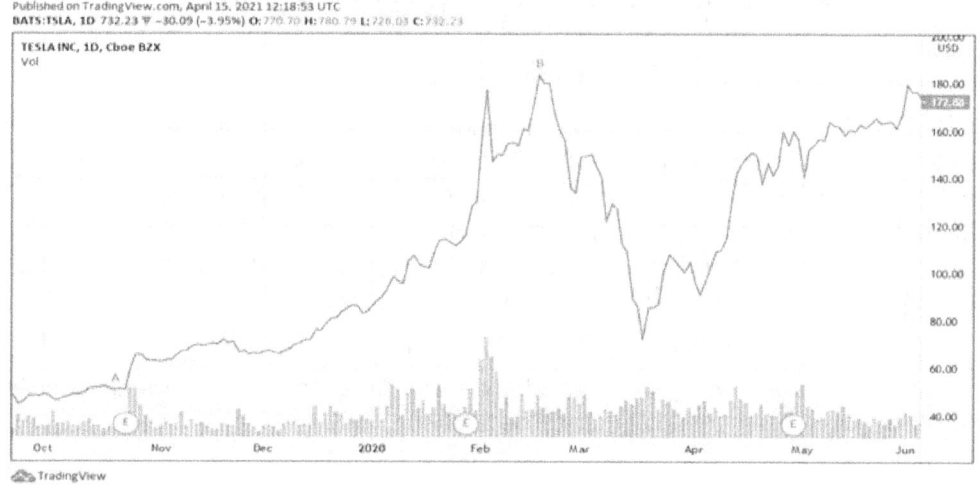

The price increase during this period must have been driven primarily by short sellers covering their positions. As they bought more Tesla stock, it was inevitable that it would rise. Looking at the short interest chart above shows that the number of shorted shares dropped while the price increased. The number of shorted shares stabilized from March 2020 to May 2020.

Based on the float of Tesla stock at the time, short sellers alone wouldn't have driven this stock to such heights. Potentially, institutional investors like investment banks held about 74% of Tesla's shares. It is likely these investors also bought more Tesla shares, and that way helped drive its stock price upwards. According to CNN Business, investors that short Tesla during 2020 lost in the vicinity of $40 billion.

This concludes Part 1. You are now ready to head over to Part 2.

Part 2

Chapter 6: The Beginning of the GameStop Saga

GameStop, a company operating in the video game retail industry, made financial news early in 2021. It became a target of short sellers. In a surprising turn of events, the bulls came charging and began to buy GameStop stock in large numbers. Eventually, the stock price began to rally, and several hedge funds incurred astronomical losses. From this chapter and onwards, we'll turn our attention to this GameStop short squeeze fiasco. But first, we need to understand GameStop, the company, so that we have a factual perspective on what might actually have happened behind the scenes to lead to the short squeeze. Furthermore, we will, later on, explore what the short squeeze means to the stock market and its participants going forward.

The History of GameStop

Image by Ricarda Mölck from Pixabay

GameStop is the largest video game retailer worldwide and has over 5,700 stores in 14 countries headquartered in Grapevine, Texas. Customers go to GameStop stores to trade and buy pre-used games. The company also sells POP! vinyl figures, collectibles, and licensed merchandise. The changing business climate has necessitated GameStop to adjust its business strategy over the years to incorporate digital in its business model. It operates www.gamestop.com and a digital magazine called *Game Informer*, available in both print and digital versions.

GameStop's history includes names most people have never heard of before. One of the most important foundations of the company was Babbage's Inc., an entity founded by two former Harvard Business School classmates James McCurry and Gary Kusin. The pair had ideas of starting a business together upon graduation from Harvard. However, that didn't happen. McCurry joined Bain & Company's San Francisco office as a consultant, while Kusin worked as a general merchandise manager for Federated Department Stores.

Only in 1982 did the former classmates meet again to discuss the possible formation of a business. McCurry had proposed that they start a chain to sell software in order to take advantage of the growing computer and home video retail sector. Kusin liked the idea. At the end of that year, these partners left their employers to launch their business. They began by looking for startup finances to get their business off the ground.

Unfortunately, they found no venture capitalist who was willing to risk their money on the startup. Not long thereafter, in February 1983, actually, the two met Ross Perot, billionaire and founder of Electronic Data Systems, who offered them $3 million. However, he wanted a one-third stake in exchange for his investment. Not only did Perot finance the startup, but he also advised McCurry and Kusin to shelve their idea of opening 20 stores and focus on just one outlet. His rationale was that the enthusiastic entrepreneurs should first learn the business inside and out before expanding it. The best way, therefore, was to open just one store and use it to sharpen their business strategy and operations.

Armed with money and savvy advice, Kusin and McCurry started preparations to launch their business. Within two months of opening their first Babbage's store, the pair nailed their sales targets and hired Mary Evans. From the foundation that had been laid, Evans helped open four additional Babbage's outlets in the Dallas area. In its first full year of operations, Babbage's made sales worth $3 million but ran at a loss of $500,000.

However, in 1986, the company broke even with $10 million in revenue and 23 stores. The expansion was financed through private sales of Babbage's stock. In 1987, sales grew to $29 million while earnings stood at $1.16 million from 35 stores. Encouraged by the growth of the company and wanting to expand further, the founders of Babbage's took the company public in July 1988. That year, revenue doubled to $58 million, and earnings rose sharply to $2.7 million, a rise of 136% compared to 1987.

A year later, Babbage's was hit by losses in the first three quarters of the year. This performance forced the company to adjust its business strategy, and they introduced a new entertainment system and software. The approach helped the business to turn around its fortunes and make a $2.3 million profit from a $95 million revenue.

Fast-forward to 1993, Babbage's opened 56 news stores, and sales rose 12% from the prior year. However, earnings fell 36% to $4.3 million, a first for the business where earnings did not match revenues. From 1994, the company began to grow through various strategies such as merging with similar businesses. For example, Babbage's merged with Software Etc. to form NeoStar Retail Group almost as a result of necessity.

At the start of 1994, Babbage's was in a good business position because it had 300 stores, no long-term debt, and boasted a cash surplus of $10.5 million. However, competition increased from various companies running software specialty stores, toy stores, and mass merchandisers such as Walmart. To stay competitive and remain in business, Babbage's entered into the merger mentioned above. McCurry was appointed as board chairman and chief executive officer (CEO), while Kusin remained president and chief operating officer (COO) until he left the company in February 1995.

NeoStar introduced new generation video game systems in 1995 to meet the challenge from the competition. Mass market giants Walmart and Best Buy had raised their game in the video gaming industry. However, the impact from the new gaming systems did not have the impact the company was looking for. NeoStar made a profit of only $120,000 from $513.5 million in sales in the financial year ending January 1996. The following quarter's performance was down because sales dipped by nine percent while the company made a loss of $8.3 million.

It was time to relook at the business. Not surprisingly, the company reorganized, and some members of the senior management team resigned. Babbage's, Software Etc., and leased software departments operating within Barnes & Noble bookstores were combined into one company and headed by Alan Bush, who was a former president of Tandy Corporation's Computer City division. Prior to this move, the three stores operated separately while being part of NeoStar as the holding company. Shortly after the reorganization, NeoStar filed for Chapter 11 bankruptcy in September 1996 amid a continued decline in sales. Thomas Plaskett, a board member, took over the chairmanship for the reorganization mainly because of his expertise in turning companies around.

In October 1996, NeoStar decided to close 42 stores located close to competing stores. Failure to secure funding for this move resulted in a sale of the company to an investor group led by Leonard Riggio, founder and then chairman of Barnes & Noble and chairman of NeoStar's executive committee. Riggio created Babbage's Etc. LLC as a holding company to operate 467 Babbage's and Software Etc. stores. Furthermore, the company closed down 200 stores. The two chains began to sell a similar mix of video game and software titles.

In the late 1990s, Babbage's returned to double-digit growth following improved operational strategies and the introduction of a 64-bit Nintendo system. As a result of the growth, in 1999, the company opened 20 new stores operating at strip malls and gave them the name GameStop. Furthermore, Babbage's introduced a website called www.thegamestop.com, later renamed www.gamestop.com, a name it maintains to this day.

In the next few months, Riggio and his group of investors sold Babbage's Etc. to Barnes & Noble for $215 million, which was three times more than what they had paid for it three years earlier. Barnes & Noble soon bought 400 FuncoLand video and computer game stores for $161.5 million. This move strengthened Babbage's move into strip malls and brought its expertise in selling high markup used games. Nearly 40% of its sales came from the sale of used games. FuncoLand also brought with it *Game Informer*, one of the top magazines in the video game industry. The deal was structured so that Babbage's became a 100% subsidiary of FuncoLand.

In December 2000, FuncoLand was renamed GameStop Inc. The following year, the company increased the number of its stores to over 1,000. Right about that time, new game systems were being introduced in the industry, and GameStop began to perform better. The number of installed gaming units in the United States was increasing at a rapid rate. From the year 2000 to 2002, the number of video games installed reached 65.1 million.

Barnes & Noble saw an opportunity to cash in. That's when they decided to incorporate GameStop Corp. in August 2001 to prepare for an initial public offering (IPO). An attempt to list on the Nasdaq in the fall of 2001 did not work out. However, the following year in February, GameStop Corp. was successfully listed on the New York Stock Exchange. In the process, it sold 20.8 million shares at $18 per share. Thus, the company raised $375.4 million from the IPO. Barnes & Noble controlled a 67% stake in GameStop at the time.

Expansion of the company continued through new store openings and resulted in GameStop making $1.58 billion in revenue and $68.5 million in profits. This was the best year ever for the company up to that time. Uncharacteristically, GameStop made profits in every quarter of 2003. In the same year, the company was taken offshore, and it acquired a controlling share in Ireland's Gamesworld Group Limited. Following this move, GameStop paid $111.5 million to buy its independence from Barnes & Noble. Going forward, the major threat to the success of GameStop remained tough competition.

Over the coming years, GameStop grew through primarily mergers and acquisitions. For example, in 2005, it merged with EB Games to create a retail chain with over 4,300 stores worldwide. Subsequently, GameStop sales came in at over $5 billion, a growth of 72% compared to the previous financial year. Net earnings increased by 57% partly as a result of introducing new video game software and next-generation consoles. Long-term debt, as of February 3, 2007, stood at $242.8 million.

By now, you should be familiar with GameStop as a business and its exciting history. Now, I don't want to bore you with more financial statement analysis. Instead, I want to jump to 2019 and 2020, the two years prior to hedge funds shorting this company to uncommon proportions. Part of the reason is that the company made a decision that might have irked investors. In 2019, GameStop boasted over 5,500 stores across the United States, Canada, Australia, and Europe.

Its net sales dipped from $8.29 billion in 2018 to $6.47 billion in 2019, which was nearly a 22% decline. A drop in net sales translated into a net loss of $470.9 million, which was better than the 2018 net loss of $673 million. Anyone reading what I have just said would wonder why the business didn't do well in 2018 and 2019. GameStop provided reasons. One of the reasons was that the company had closed 321 stores globally as part of its efforts to build a stronger business.

The second reason pertained to lower demand for consoles from Sony and Microsoft as the current versions were nearing the end of their lifecycle. Another factor contributing to the results was that software sales, audio-related products, and other accessories declined due to growth in battle-royal gaming and a lower number and success of title releases versus in 2018.

Before we look at GameStop's performance in 2020, let's analyze how its stock was performing coming up to 2019. The table below shows earnings per share from 2015 to 2019 as well as dividends GameStop paid out to stockholders in the same period. The data used below comes from GameStop's 2019 annual report.

	2015	2016	2017	2018	2019
Earnings per share ($)	3.55	2.93	2.27	-7.79	-5.31
Dividend per share ($)	1.44	1.48	1.52	1.52	0.38

It is clear that earnings per share were declining from 2015 to 2017 before the company made losses in the 2018 and 2019 financial years. This is a sign that the business was facing operational challenges that needed to be addressed. Some of the challenges were mentioned above in the 2019 analysis of GameStop's financial performance. GameStop paid dividends consistently from 2015 to 2018, except that the amount stayed the same from 2017 to 2018. This deviated from a rising trend of paying dividends from 2015 to 2017. In 2019, GameStop eliminated quarterly dividends to continue to further reduce debt and strengthen the asset row in the balance sheet.

How did the above fundamentals translate to GameStop's stock performance? This company looked at how its stock performed from 2015 to 2019 financial years compared to the S&P 500 and Dow Jones Specialty Retailers Index. Below is the comparison, assuming you put $100 in each and also reinvested dividends. The data sourced from GameStop's 2019 annual report.

	1/30/ 2015	1/29/ 2016	1/29/ 2017	2/2/ 2018	2/1/ 2019	1/31/ 2020
GameStop ($)	100.00	77.09	75.38	54.07	41.41	14.64
S&P 500 ($)	100.00	99.33	120.04	147.44	147.35	179.10
Dow Jones Specialty Index ($)	100.00	103.02	119.63	153.96	176.49	193.73

From the data, if you invested $100 in GameStop in 2015, its value would have declined to $14.64, a loss of $85.36 or 85.36%. However, both the S&P 500 and Dow Jones Specialty Index would have earned you $77.10 and $93.73, respectively. That's a return of 77.10% and 93.73% return over the five years, respectively. Purely based on this data, GameStop as a stock did not do well for investors going long on it over the period analyzed. The chart below represents the data graphically for further clarity of the comparison.

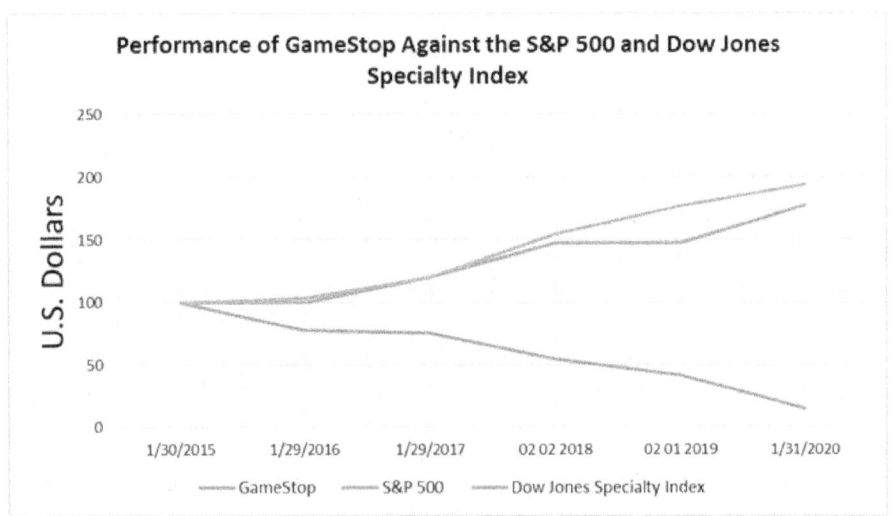

In their 2019 annual report, GameStop had this to say in the overview of their financial results:

> The near-term global economic conditions have been adversely impacted by the emergence of a novel coronavirus in China, identified as COVID-19, which continues to spread throughout the United States and other parts of the world. In March 2020, the World Health Organization declared the outbreak of COVID-19 as a pandemic. In an effort to mitigate the continued spread of the virus, governments have imposed quarantines, travel restrictions, and similar measures. We have temporarily closed stores on a country-wide basis in Europe, primarily in Italy and France, as well as in Canada, which became effective in various points in March 2020. In the United States, effective March 22, 2020, we have temporarily closed all storefronts to customers but continue to process orders on a digital only basis, offering curbside pick-up at stores and e-commerce delivery only. As a result of these actions and restrictions, we expect a significant reduction in customer traffic and demand.

Despite a dismal performance in the 2019 financial year, GameStop mentioned that Sony and Microsoft were due to release their next-generation consoles during the 2020 holiday season. This, together with the fact that sales of online products were increasing, boded well for the company.

We now turn our attention to the performance of GameStop in 2020. Instead of reviewing the performance over the whole year, we'll go through the results of each quarter. We'll conclude by bringing the quarterly results together to evaluate the whole year's performance. The aim of this exercise is to provide a background into what transpired prior to heavy shorting of GameStop. At the same time, this information will help any investor learn to evaluate a company before they invest in it. A savvy investor should not rely on third-party analysis for their investment decisions. So, it's absolutely necessary to learn how the investing process works, particularly the evaluation of a business, in order to decide whether to invest in it or not.

Now, let's continue and see how GameStop performed during its 2020 financial year. The numbers quoted here are from quarterly results that GameStop released during and as the year progressed. As this company had expected, it registered a loss of $165.7 million dollars in the first quarter of 2020. The main reason for the loss was a temporary closure of 3,526 of its stores in the United States due to COVID-19 restrictions. To mitigate the losses, GameStop instituted a curbside pick-up offering at 65% of its stores.

On the positive side, GameStop saw a surge in its e-commerce sales, which jumped by 519% compared to a similar period in the previous year. Unfortunately, GameStop could not offer any 2020 outlook due to uncertainties surrounding COVID-19 and its potential impact on its business operations. Losses continued in the second quarter as GameStop saw a net loss of $111.3 million, an improvement compared to the previous quarter by nearly $64 million. This was also an improvement compared to the same period in 2019, where the company netted losses of $415.3 million.

Online sales continued to soar as GameStop recorded an 800% increase during the quarter. This improvement resulted in e-commerce sales contributing to over a fifth of GameStop's net sales. The downward slide in financial performance didn't end in the second quarter. GameStop continued to make net losses in the third quarter of 2020 as it recorded a net loss of $18.8 million. That was a decrease in net loss by almost $93 million compared to the previous quarter, and it was better than a 2019 third-quarter loss of $83.4 million. Online sales continued to surge as they advanced 257% relative to a similar period in the previous year. GameStop expected to make a profit in the next quarter owing to the introduction of new-generation gaming consoles.

Yes, it did make a positive profit. The amount recorded in the fourth quarter was $80.5 million, which was lower than the comparable period in 2019 by $3.3 million. E-commerce sales kept improving and came in at a rise of 175% and contributed 34% to net sales versus 12% in the same period in 2019.

Overall, in 2020, GameStop made sales of $5.090 billion compared to $6.466 billion in the previous year. This video retailer attributed the drop to a 12% decrease in its store base and a temporary closure of some of its stores due to COVID-19. The impact of COVID-19 was offset by an increase in global online sales of 191% for the year, which represented nearly 30% of net sales.

Net losses came in at $215.3 million, an improvement compared to a net loss of $470.9 million in 2019. Some of the positive news from GameStop included reducing total debt to $462.7 million. Furthermore, this business ended the year having $635 million of cash in hand, an increase of about $122 million versus 2019. Although GameStop did not produce sterling results in 2020, signs of improvement were there throughout the year. Now, how do investors decide to short a business whose fundamentals seemed to improve?

Further positive news coming from the GameStop camp revealed that three new board members were added, including Ryan Cohen. I'll give you a profile of Ryan Cohen later in this chapter. For now, suffice it to say Ryan Cohen owns about 12.9% of GameStop's floating stock through his firm RC Ventures, making him the single largest shareholder in the company.

Why Did Hedge Funds Short GameStop?

As you may have realized from the analysis of GameStop, the business relies primarily on physical video game hardware and software. However, this company began to perform poorly from 2018 to 2019. Things started to improve as the 2020 year wore on because GameStop had to drive its online sales. Having said that, should GameStop stock have been shorted excessively? It seems there is a widespread belief that GameStop's business model was wrong—that it relied too much on physical games when the world was shifting to online game playing. The question we should ask is, "Is this perspective true? If so, is the only reason for shorting GameStop stock so much?"

Andrew Left, head of Citron Research, came out strongly to support the theory that GameStop deserves to be short. A January 26, 2021 article on Reuters quoted him as having said, "If I had never been involved in GameStop and came to this right now, would I still short this stock? (Hundred) 100 percent. This is an old school, failing mall-based video retailer, and investors can't change the perception of that."

Based on this assessment, Left borrowed shares to short GameStop when it was trading at about $40 a share. At the time he made the bet, Left had predicted that the publicly traded video retailer's share would drop to $20 per share. At this time of Left's prediction, hedge funds had not been short squeezed yet.

Melvin Capital Management, a fund management company, shorted GameStop through share put options for four quarters in a row in 2020. This became clear based on their filing with the SEC. Melvin had shorted GameStop with 2.8 million shares in the first quarter, 3.4 million in the second quarter, 5.4 million in the third quarter, and finally, 6 million in the fourth quarter. The last filing amounted to a holding of around $113 million, as revealed in the regulatory filing.

Melvin founder, Gabe Plotkin, revealed that he had been shorting GameStop since 2014 but provided no reason for doing so. However, like Andrew Left, he believes that GameStop's business model is outdated as it is being outpaced by digital downloads of video games. Was this the same reason that Plotkin's firm had been shorting GameStop since 2014?

Findings from Think with Google, in partnership with OC & C Strategy Consultants, seem to agree with Left's and Plotkin's perspectives on the direction of the video game industry. The investigation was intended to identify developments in the video game industry that might be driving the market. They concluded that digital sales and distribution continued to grow while physical game sales were declining. Factors that they cited for this shift included improved internet speeds, widespread use of smartphones, and availability of large storage volumes in modern hardware.

While this may be true, human nature changes slowly. How long did it take for a large number of people to use computers? According to Statista, 27.1% of households worldwide used computers compared to 47.1% in 2019. This is nearly a 100% increase in about 14 years. Still, only about half of households are using computers. The point I want to get across is that a shift often occurs slowly. We can expect people to migrate from physical video games to digital versions steadily. In that respect, GameStop can still adjust its business model to prepare and take advantage of this shift.

The year 2020 proved to be one where GameStop was 'forced' to innovate due to COVID-19. Ryan Cohen and the two other new board members were brought on board to help this company make this shift faster. Despite this clear shift in direction, hedge funds continued to hold onto their short positions, hoping to cash in from the collapse of GameStop. For further evidence of the intention of GameStop to modify or change its business model, we go back to its financial performance and notice that its online sales grew to just over a third of its total net sales by the end of its 2020 financial year. We must acknowledge that online sales are not large enough to shift the direction of this company's revenue. However, this could be something to be expected in the next few years.

Commenting on the announcement of GameStop's partnership with Microsoft in October 2020, George Sherman, CEO of GameStop, said, "This is an exciting day for GameStop as we announce the advancement of an important partnership that capitalizes on the power of our operating platform and significant market share in gaming to accelerate our digital transformation; drive incremental revenue streams; and over time, further monetize the digital world of gaming."

You have to wonder why hedge funds, even after seeing clear signs of GameStop wanting to beat a new path, kept hanging onto their short positions. It is a difficult idea, though, to comprehend. What's fascinating is that there were hedge funds and professional funds that went long on GameStop. One such hedge fund is Senvest Management, a firm founded by Richard Mashaal in 1997 and headquartered in New York, boasting $3 billion in assets under management (AUM). The company prides itself on its contrarian and value-based approach to investments.

Mr. Mashaal and Senvest had developed an interest in GameStop at a consumer investment conference in January 2020. GameStop had just hired a new CEO, and he was making his first presentation for the company. At that time, analysts had rated GameStop as either a 'hold' or a 'sell.' Not surprising, the GameStop stock was heavily sold. Later, Senvest became aware that certain hedge funds such as Melvin Capital Management had taken bearish positions on GameStop.

After doing their homework, that is, researching GameStop's competition, speaking to management, and evaluating investors' activity on the stock, Senvest bought shares in the company. This was a classic case of the contrarian approach Senvest favors considering that other similar firms were bearish on GameStop. At the close of October 2020, Senvest owned over 5% (or 3.6 million shares) of GameStop and had paid around $10 per share for the majority of their holdings. Their reason for investing in GameStop, Senvest argued, was that if the video game retailer could survive until new consoles hit the shelves, its stock would trend upwards.

Senvest was not alone in its bullish sentiments on GameStop. BlackRock Inc. filed a GameStop stock ownership equivalent to 13.2% (or 9.2 million shares) of float. This was actually a reduction in exposure from 18.23% to 13.2%. As of January 10, 2021, the top ten institutional investors in GameStop held about 77.5% of GameStop's float. Here's a summary of each institutional investor's holding by April 13, 2021, according to GameStop.

Holder	Shares Held	% O/S	Filing Date
Fidelity Management & Research Company LLC	9,276,087	13.3	12/31/20
RC Ventures LLC	9,001,000	12.91	1/10/21

BlackRock Institutional Trust Company, N.A.	8,489,953	12.17	12/31/20
The Vanguard Group, Inc.	5,162,095	7.4	12/31/20
Senvest Management, LLC	5,050,915	7.24	12/31/20
Maverick Capital, Ltd.	4,658,607	6.68	12/31/20
Dimensional Fund Advisors, L.P.	3,934,919	5.64	12/31/20
Morgan Stanley Investment Management Inc. (US)	3,168,279	4.54	12/31/20
D. E. Shaw & Co., L.P.	2,841,563	4.07	12/31/20
Susquehanna International Group, LLP	2,487,366	3.57	12/31/20

Amid mixed feelings towards GameStop, one man became one of the major stockholders in the company. His name is Ryan Cohen, who founded chewy.com, a pet food and toy company. He had started the company with a $15 million capital from a venture capitalist. Three years later, in 2016, Chewy raised $230 million and went on to make $900 million in sales that year. The following, Chewy raised $350 million before being bought by PetSmart for $3.35 billion. PetSmart took Chewy public in 2019, and the pet food company now has a market capitalization of about $43 billion.

The developments at Chewy explained above pocketed Cohen several hundred million dollars. In August 2020, Cohen filed his share ownership in GameStop with the SEC. It had been unknown that besides acquiring shares in Apple and Wells Fargo, Cohen had been buying shares in the strip mall video game retailer. As you can see in the table above, Cohen owns just over 9 million shares, through RC Ventures LLC, estimated to have cost him $8 a share for a total spend of around $76 million. Cohen made important moves to try and get GameStop to accelerate its transformation to the digital space and dominate the gaming world. You'll still hear about him in the next chapter.

Chapter 7: The Major GameStop Short Squeeze

In this chapter, we are going to analyze the events that may have led to investors buying GameStop in numbers. The reason is that at some point, the bulls overpowered the bears, and a major short squeeze occurred. We have already discussed GameStop and possible reasons the bears shorted it. The basic reason, as you may recall, was that the business was headed for bankruptcy. This idea was strengthened at some point when the company went for sale recently. However, no one came forward to buy GameStop. I have no doubt that the biggest player in this short squeeze was the financial performance and business outlook of GameStop. All the rest of the things that happened were reactions to this factor.

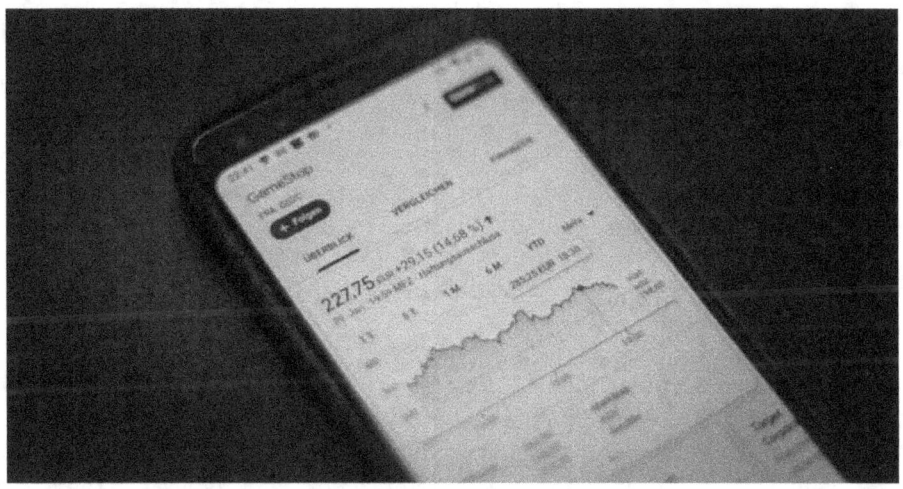

Image by Michael Förtsch on Unsplash

We'll start with the first trigger of the GameStop short squeeze, which happened in 2019 while the business was struggling to make money. In came a hedge fund manager named Michael Burry, who founded and runs Scion Asset Management. Let's look at what he did.

The Role of Michael Burry in the GameStop Short Squeeze

Let's start by looking at who Michael Burry is before we go into the details of his actions regarding GameStop. Michael Burry is a qualified medical doctor trained at the Vanderbilt University's School of Medicine. He took up his medical studies following his studies of economics and pre-med at the University of California. While doing his residency at Stanford Hospital, Burry would spend time studying financial investments. From this side work, he began to invest and also created a blog where he shared his stock market ideas, trends, and investing tips.

In 2000, he quit his medical career and started Scion Asset Management, an investment firm. The confidence to start such a business came from the attention Burry was receiving from high-profile fund managers and investment banks. He was later diagnosed with Asperger Syndrome, a disorder that influences how a person socializes and communicates with others. Burry communicated with investors in his company via letters to keep them informed about the performance of their investments.

Burry's approach to investing is summed up in articles that he wrote and published on MSN Money. John Chew of csinvesting.org organized those articles as case studies for investors to learn from. Here's how Burry describes his investing strategy or philosophy. I have italicized points I want you to pay attention to.

> My strategy isn't very complex. I try *to buy shares of unpopular companies when they look like roadkill*, and sell them when they've been polished up a bit. Management of my portfolio as a whole is just as important to me as stock picking, and if I can do both well, I know I'll be successful.
>
> My weapon of choice as a stock picker is research; *it's critical for me to understand a company's value before laying down a dime.* I really had no choice in this matter, for when I first happened upon the writings of Benjamin Graham, I felt as if I was born to play the role of value investor. *All my stock picking is 100% based on the concept of a margin of safety*, as introduced to the world in the book "Security Analysis," which Graham co-authored with David Dodd. By now, I have my own version of their techniques, but the net is that *I want to protect my downside to prevent permanent loss of capital.* Specific, known catalysts are not necessary. *Sheer, outrageous value is enough.*

It's clear that Burry is a value investor. He looks for value in a business before he invests in a company. As you may know, value investing is an approach touted by greats such as Warren Buffet, who himself was a student of Benjamin Graham. Michael Burry became popular when Michael Lewis featured him in the book *The Big Short* following the housing bubble of 2007-2008. Burry had successfully forecasted and shorted the real estate market that led to that financial crisis and pocketed him around $100 million and his investors $700 million.

With this backdrop, we can understand why Burry bought 536,862 shares in GameStop, estimated to be worth around $7 million at that time (late 2018). In the first quarter of 2019, Burry added 113,138 to his long position to take it to 650,000 shares. However, he liquidated all his shares by the end of quarter two in 2019. You'll recall that GameStop was making net losses in 2018 and 2019. Yet, one of the savvy value investors had decided to go long on the company. Why would he do that? Based on his investment philosophy introduced above, we can conclude that he must have seen value in GameStop.

Interestingly, Burry reinvested in GameStop when his fund bought approximately 3 million shares. Soon after, the Scion fund manager wrote a letter to the video game retailer's board of directors. The letter was to be one of the important pieces of documentation that influenced certain investors to go long on GameStop. Let me not get ahead of myself. Burry was clear about what he thought the business should do to win back investor confidence and put the company in a good financial position.

In the letter mentioned above, Burry said that he was concerned about the manner in which the leadership of GameStop managed its capital. He believed that GameStop had an opportunity to buy back $237.6 million worth of company shares. His idea was to influence the company to retire 80% of its outstanding shares and increase its earnings per share and any other per share measurable.

Burry said something in the above-mentioned letter that, unknowingly at that time, may have caught the attention of some retail investors. At least one investor caught the significance of this letter, and his name is Keith Gill. We'll talk about his involvement in a short while. Here's what I believe Burry said that might have kicked off a buying frenzy in the GameStop stock.

"We expect GameStock's business will perk up a bit during 2020 and 2021 as the new console cycle, with associated software updates and introductions, finally gets underway." Burry went on and said, "But what is happening now in the stock is about more than late cycle doldrums or even the streaming paradigm—shareholders do not have faith in current management and have not been inspired by new leadership policies." Although the latter statement sounds bearish, it has a connotation that says the business has value, only that the leaders of GameStop are not able to extract it. We know that later there were management changes in the company. Coronavirus, in early 2020, didn't help as governments had to implement measures to handle its spread. This news was not helpful for a business model based on physical stores, and GameStop was not spared.

Besides Michael Burry, there was another prominent role player in the GameStop short squeeze. He operated in the world of a social media platform known as Reddit. We are going to follow his moves from around late 2019 until the short squeeze occurred.

Wallstreetbets Investing Teachers

Before we detail what Keith Gill did, let us briefly talk about a subreddit called Wallstreetbets. It is an important role player in this fiasco that we are unraveling. The forum was founded in 2012 by Jaime Rogozinski, who claimed that he saw a major short squeeze coming. A Mexico City resident, Rogozinski believes Wallstreetbets accomplished what Occupy Wall Street attempted but failed to achieve.

To him, the intention of his subreddit forum has always been to shift power from Wall Street to Main Street. The members of the forum share trading and investing tips. However, their main drive is to make money in the short term through financial instruments such as stock options and other derivatives. Wallstreetbets is for investors eager to challenge the status quo in the financial world in a less formal environment.

One member of Wallstreetbets is Keith Gill, who goes by the name DeepF***gValue. For simplicity, many members of the forum call him DFV. The 34-year-old lives in Boston. Before becoming popular due to the GameStop short squeeze, Gill worked for Massachusetts Mutual Life Insurance Company. He developed an interest in the stock market after college and saw it as an opportunity to make extra cash. Furthermore, he enjoyed the complexity and challenge of picking stocks. Like Michael Burry, Gill's investing philosophy hinges on selecting stocks that are out of favor and undervalued.

Little did Gill know that his investing philosophy, timing, and I believe also a bit of luck would turn his GameStop investment into a dream investment. According to posts he made on Reddit, Gill began sharing a snapshot of his investments in GameStop on September 8, 2019.

I need to make something clear up front. Gill did not buy GameStop common stock to invest in its business. Instead, he bought call options. On September 8, 2019, he had 1,000 contracts and had paid $53,566.04 for them on average. What caught my attention was the headline of the post, which said, "Hey Burry Thanks a lot for jacking up my cost basis." This was followed by a tag called YOLO, meaning you live only once. Almost all the headlines on his posts were followed by this tag. I must mention that some members of Wallstreetbets derided Gill for taking long positions on GameStop especially at the start. The information I am sharing with you about Gill and his investments mostly comes from the Wallstreetbets forum.

Gill updated the Wallstreetbets forum about the progress of his trading account at the end of each month. However, sometimes he posted more than once a month. By the end of December 2019, his account had just over $112,000 in total with $22,300.13 in cash. Obviously, Gill had increased his position progressively to reach this level. Even when

GameStop's stock price dipped after they announced depressed quarter-three results of 2019, Gill added to his existing positions instead of selling. One member of Wallstreetbets responded to Gill's update showing he added to his position by saying, "You honestly have a better chance playing roulette."

In January and February 2020, DFV's account was covered in red numbers, suggesting that GameStop stock was performing poorly. At the end of February, Gill had $183.83 in cash and a total account value of $44,483.83. This decline in total value means that he had lost over 100% of the account's value compared to December 2019. What would you have done if you were Keith Gill at that time? Most would probably have thrown in the towel.

That's exactly what DFV did not do. The next time he posted an update was on April 14, 2020. Astonishingly, the GameStop stock price had gone from around $3.25 on April 12th to nearly $5.94 on April 15th as shown in the chart below. The stock had risen by nearly 83%. It was on this day that DFV mentioned, for the first time, the possibility of a GameStop short squeeze when he posted, "GME YOLO update following the start of the Big Short Squeeze."

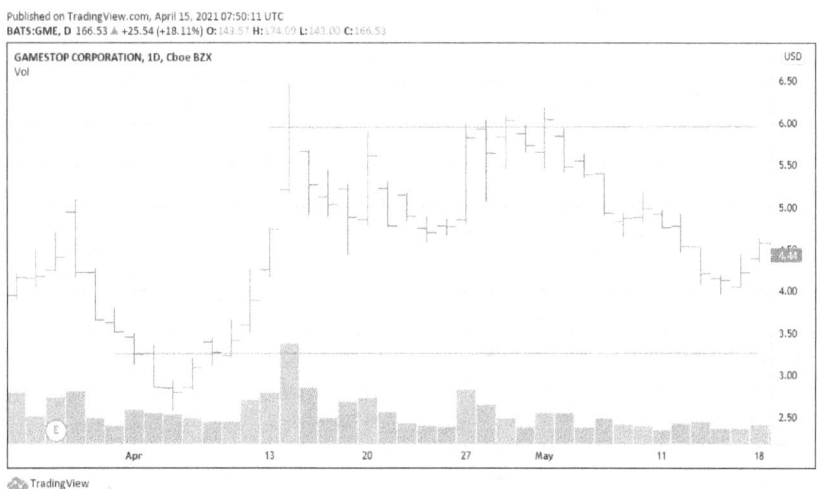

At that time, his GameStop investment was worth $298,400 with almost $104,000 in cash. His possible reason for a GameStop short squeeze stemmed from the fact that its stock's short interest was 123.64% at the time. This means that there was heavy short selling of GameStop at that time. So, a big increase in the stock's price, Gill must have thought, would force some short sellers to close their positions. In the process, they would have pushed the stock price further up and squeezing out more short sellers. The important question to ask is, "Why did GameStop stock price rise that much?" Ponder on that question for a minute.

We'll come back to Keith Gill's posts shortly. I want us to consider, because of the timing of his post, another Wallstreetbets investing teacher called Senior_Hedgehog. (At the time of this writing, the real identity of Senior_Hedgehog was unknown.) The reason is that this member added a post around April 2020 regarding GameStop stock as a steal to buy. And, there were interesting points this individual pointed out that are material to the occurrence of the GameStop short squeeze. The title of the post that Senior_Hedgehog wrote said, "GameStop (GME)—THE BIGGEST SHORT SQUEEZE OF YOUR ENTIRE LIFE."

Then, Senior_Hedgehog made four points they believed made GameStop stock a buy and a potential candidate for a big short squeeze. Let's go over each of them.

- Senior_Hedgehog noted that GameStop had 65.5 million shares, and 55 million of these shares were shorted. That represented 84% of shares that were short. They went on to say that Michael Burry owned 3.5 million shares long and encouraged the readers to look up proxy war. Senior_Hedgehog's evaluation centered around a high short interest in GameStop stock and that big players were interested in going long on the stock.

- They mentioned that GameStop tended to make the most money when new consoles entered the market. Of course, Senior_Hedgehog based this idea on what happened in the past. What's more telling is what they said next—that often the stock jumps up by an average of over 120% during new console releases. In effect, Senior_Hedgehog was saying that anyone who bought GameStop stock early could see their shares growing by over 120% within a few weeks. Who wouldn't want to get such returns, especially a Wallstreetbets member?

- One of the most important statistics they added pointed out that gaming consumption was estimated to rise by 75%. Again, this suggests that more demand for GameStop wares would drive revenue and, potentially, its stock upwards.

- The last point indicated that games require large memory, and console hard drives cannot handle them. For that reason, Senior_Hedgehog believed there might be a return to the use of disk games.

In concluding their argument for GameStop stock, Senior_Hedgehog made this point in uppercase letters: "If you are long, make sure to call in your shares from your broker and make sure they aren't being short-lent (call your brokers)." Unfortunately, while writing this book, someone deleted the original post. Only the title of the post remains with a note explaining why the post was removed.

A look at the comments that followed revealed that some members of the Wallstreetbets forum began to buy call options on the GameStop stock. One user, "aidank1234" responded by saying, "Shoutout to you bro, my GME $6.50c 4/17 more than doubled this morning before I sold." Senior_Hedgehog replied, "Congrats but you shouldn't of (have) sold you might regret that."

Like with DFV, not everyone on the forum agreed with Senior_Hedgehog. For example, one member commented on the latter's post by saying, "'Games have increased memory size and the console hard drives can't handle them.' All I needed to see to know that I need to do the opposite of what you are advocating." This comment and many others have since been removed as well.

Wallstreetbets wasn't the only place where perspectives on GameStop were shared. After Michael Burry's letters to the board of GameStop, a writer by the name of Napoleon Capital wrote a piece on GameStop. The article appeared on Seeking Alpha on August 20, 2019. Napoleon Capital describes itself as a full-time finance student who invests in their spare time. The article warned that "Shorting GameStop is a dangerous game."

Capital was not optimistic about the long-term prospects of GameStop. In fact, they thought that the video game retailer was heading the way of Blockbuster, a former provider of home video rentals. Their reason for not shorting GameStop? Capital feared the potential of a major short squeeze. In their own words, Capital said, "The main reason I'm staying away is that being short GameStop stock is an extremely crowded trade, and the potential for a major short squeeze is high. With over 55% of outstanding shares and 90+% of float sold short, it is one of the most shorted stocks on the market."

What was telling were Capital's thoughts that the GameStop stock price already accounted for the company's poor performance. You can read this to mean that the stock was oversold. All that needed to happen to trigger a short squeeze would be some positive news from the GameStop camp. And positive news did keep coming in 2020, heading towards 2021.

Meanwhile, Keith Gill went on to update the Wallstreetbets forum about his GameStop investment. In July 2020, he held 10,000 GME shares bought at $4.11 and 5,000 call options. The total value of the investment sat at $112,236.78, with cash amounting to $26,368.78. Fast-forward to October 8, 2020, DFV was already sitting at $2.274 million and just over $250,000 in cash. The post sharing this information garnered the most comments of any he had shared before. Reading some of the comments shows that many were seeing DFV as a hero and wanted to emulate him.

One Wallstreetbets member named "qholmes98" commented with what I believe was a reiteration of what value investors had said about the stock. Here's what they said:

I've been casually following GME since like 2018 so I can give an educated guess. Up until Cohen bought up a % of the company, there wasn't really any indication of what exactly was gonna happen in the future. But I remember value investors saying since like 2018 that GME was undervalued if you look at its asset to debt ratio or something.

So I don't think anyone knew what was going to happen, but there were people who definitely knew that there was a good opportunity for something to happen, especially with how insane the % of shares being shorted on this company is.

Once Cohen came aboard it was a perfect storm for a pop like this eventually, a dude like him doesn't just throw his money around unless he intends to make a ROI.

By the end of December 2020, Gill was sitting on a total value of over $3.1 million. The following month, January, ended with the investment having grown to around $46 million. We know that the short squeeze was on by this time. What I find interesting is that Gill spoke little throughout his Wallstreetbets posts, especially about a possible GameStop stock short squeeze. There was only one occasion when he hinted at a possible GameStop short squeeze, and that was around April 2020 or so. Yet, there are many talks suggesting that he was behind the drive to capitulate hedge funds such as Melvin Capital and Citron.

There were several accusations in the media that Gill drove the GameStop short squeeze fiasco. He may have contributed late when some members of Wallstreetbets saw his account growing by leaps and bounds. The Wall Street Journal (WSJ) interviewed Gill and published his take on the GameStop short squeeze on January 29, 2021. In the interview, Gill said that he did not go out to attract the attention of anyone, including other retail investors, hedge funds, and Congress.

One of the people on Reddit, according to the WSJ article, said, "Your steady hand convinced many of us to not only buy but hold. Your example has literally changed the lives of thousands of ordinary, normal people. Seriously thank you. You deserve every penny." Gill also shared his thoughts on GameStop stock on YouTube. He basically thought that the company was undervalued; hence, he took a bullish position on it.

Unless he had insider information that other people had no access to, I see no reason Gill could have instigated the short squeeze. Some people believe the short squeeze came about because of hatred towards Melvin Capital Management. They cite a video posted on Reddit with the title "GME Squeeze and the Demise of Melvin Capital" as evidence of their suspicion.

There are three important conditions for a short squeeze to occur. There must be a high short interest, low float, and enough buying of the stock. Clearly, had there been no high short interest, the squeeze wouldn't have happened. Similarly, a lower level of bullish actions wouldn't have created a short squeeze. The major issue is that there was high short interest on the GameStop stock for too long, and retail investors and possibly institutional investors may have bought more of the stock.

I suspect that many Wallstreetbets forum members bought GameStop because of Gill's investment performance, thinking they may emulate his performance.

I want us to revisit the GameStop stock's short interest to gauge what happened from the first quarter of 2019 to the end of March 2021. This will also include the role that other people played in setting up this big short squeeze. Here's a chart showing how short interest on the GameStop stock changed, including the stock price on the day the short interest was reported. The data used here were sourced from MarketBeat.

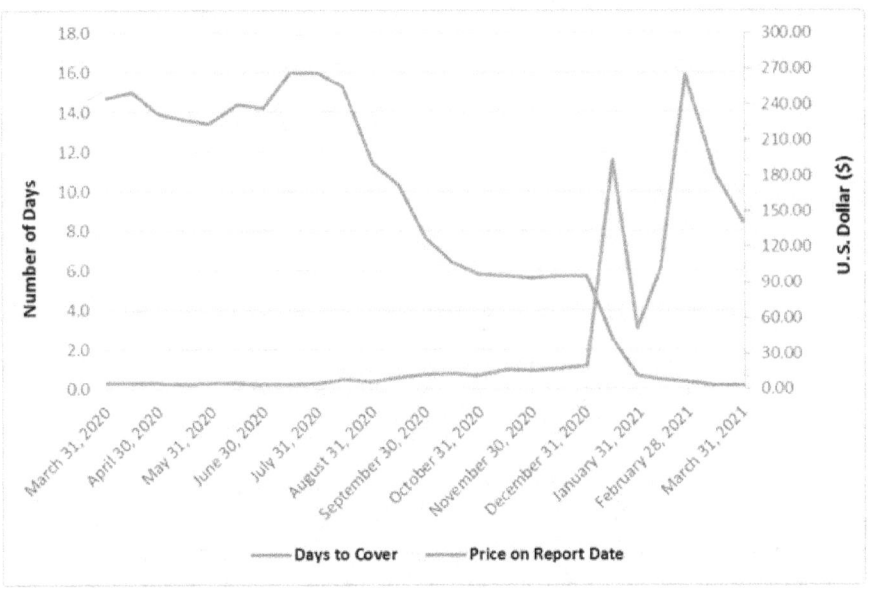

I have used the number of days-to-cover for short interest because the data was easily available. Looking at the chart above, the number of days-to-cover ranged between about 13 and 16 from March 2020 to July 31 of the same year. During the same period, GameStop stock price recorded on the day of reporting short interest was between $4 and $4.60. However, the price began to rise steadily from $4.60 to $11.88 by September 30, 2020.

During that period, short interest began to decline. The most logical reason is that Ryan Cohen had announced his shareholding in GameStop in August 2020, and the market was reacting to the news. Possibly, some hedge funds were covering their shorts, suspecting a short-term rise in the stock price that could lead to losses. However, some hedge funds such as Melvin Capital Management kept their holdings and actually increased their shorted shares to 5.4 million.

The GameStop stock price kept steadily rising until it reached around $19.94 on December 31, 2020. As can be seen in the chart, by the time the next short interest report came, the GameStop stock price had jumped to $193.60, an increase of 87% relative to the price on December 31, 2020. For actual progress in the GameStop stock price, let's have a look at its trading chart below.

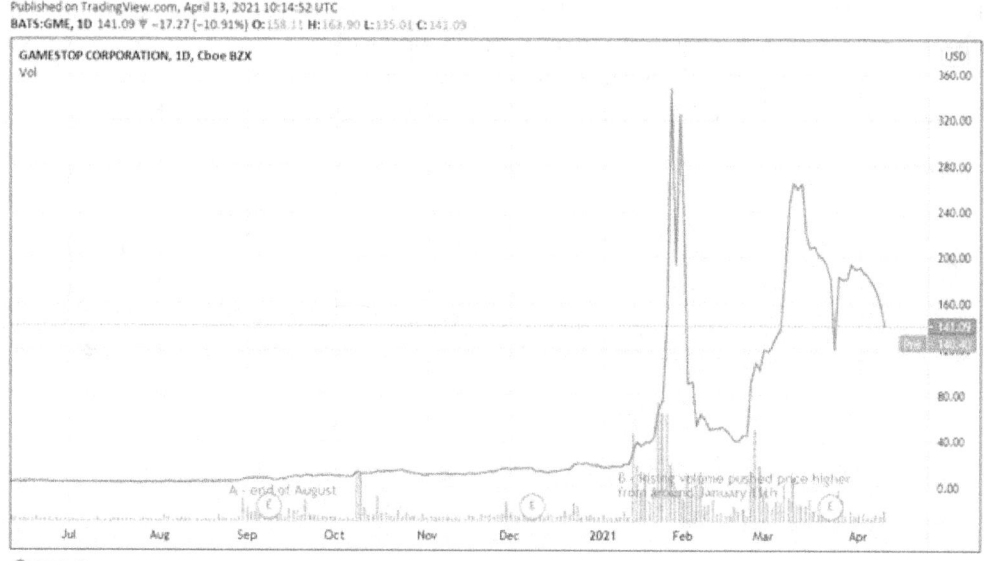

Notice point A in the chart above. It corresponds with an increase in the volume of transactions which resulted in a price increase. Since that time, the stock has not returned to those price levels. You can also see that the price began its steady rise from around August 2020. Ryan Cohen's announcement was big news for GameStop since the market probably expected him to push for a change in the company's business model. Cohen delivered the news that some investors were anticipating when he sent GameStop's board of directors a letter specifying what he wanted.

Let's briefly go over some of the important points that Cohen raised about the company and the performance of the board. Cohen's letter, dated November 16, 2020, spelled that RC Ventures LLC held 9.98% of GameStop's common stock. He urged the leadership of GameStop to review the business with the aim of snapping up opportunities that were coming thick and fast in the gaming industry. For the record, Newzoo had estimated that gamers would splash around $159.3 billion on games in 2020. They went on to say that they expected the number to skyrocket to $217.9 billion by 2023.

Without mincing his words, Cohen was clear that GameStop should become a technology company that's customer focused and stop being a traditional video game retailer. Perhaps more telling was Cohen's belief that GameStop could still bounce back and reclaim some of its market share it had forfeited to the competition. At the time, Cohen told GameStop's board that RC Ventures had no interest in the offer of a lone board member. Cohen felt one board member would not be able to have the impact that they (RC Ventures) were looking for.

Despite reporting depressed financial results throughout the remainder of the year, GameStop's stock price rose from around $6 to $19.95 by December 31, 2020. This means that the stock price rose by approximately 232% in that period. Any investor who would have shorted GameStop at $6 would have made big losses if they waited until December to close their positions. We know that certain hedge funds did not cover their shorts and remained open for further potential losses.

Beginning around January 11, 2021, we start to see the volume of transacted shares increasing extensively. Importantly, the rise in volume is accompanied by an increase in the stock price. The meaning of this is that investors were buying the stock in large numbers, and therefore, the market was predominantly bullish on the stock. In general, the volume of share transactions rose until about January 27, 2021, when the stock price jumped to about $348.12 a share. That was an increase of 2,116% from the year-opening price level of $16.45 in just 27 days. It was during the period from January 11th that certain hedge funds which had shorted GameStop felt the sting of the short squeeze.

What happened on and around January 11, 2021 in the GameStop stable? GameStop announced the inclusion of three new board members as I revealed in the previous chapter. This is what Cohen said following the appointment:

> We are excited to bring our customer-obsessed mindset and technology experience to GameStop and its strategic assets. We believe the Company can enhance stockholder value by expanding the ways in which it delights customers and by becoming the ultimate destination for gamers. Alan, Jim, and I are committed to working alongside our fellow directors and the management team to continue to transform GameStop. In addition, we intend to bring additional ownership perspectives to the boardroom.

You'll recall that in the first letter that Cohen had sent to the GameStop board that he was not interested in taking up a single board position. So, with the appointment of three board members that Cohen had worked with in the past, there is hope that the company could be transformed. Here are short biographies on Alan Attal and Jim Grube, the two new board members we have not yet profiled.

Alan Attal has over two decades as a successful e-commerce entrepreneur and executive. He was chief marketing officer of a Cohen-founded Chewy Inc., and allocated over $300 million annually to marketing Chewy. Furthermore, Attal, as chief executive officer of Chewy, helped expand the business from just three people to over 10,000 employees and $3 billion in income.

Jim Grube, like Attal, worked for Chewy as the chief financial officer from 2015 to 2018. Prior to that, he was vice-president of finance at Hilton from 2009 to 2015. He was also a former director of finance at Amazon from 2007 to 2009.

The new board of GameStop was now equipped with the necessary skills to take the business to another level through a different business model.

As you may know, hedge funds that kept their short positions on GameStop stock were soon to pay a heavy price. By January 26, 2021, GameStop stock short interest was valued at nearly $5.51 billion, with 71.79 million shares sold short, representing 139.57% of its float. Whoever was taking new short positions on GameStop stock was paying nearly an 80% fee per year (Dusaniwsky, 2021). This charge is called a stock loan fee, an amount that a brokerage firm charges anyone who borrows shares, whether a hedge fund or retail investor.

The amount you pay is based on the difficulty of borrowing a share. This is the effect of the law of supply and demand at play. The more demand there is of shares to short, the lower the supply. As a result, prices increase, and in this case, the price is the stock loan fee. With a high short interest on GameStop, it was difficult to borrow its stock. Hence, brokers probably charged the highest stock loan fee of any company in the market.

Chapter 8: The Ethics of the GameStop Fiasco

There were certain behaviors before and after the GameStop short squeeze that were questionable. Those behaviors did not seem to be ethical. I would like us to investigate some of them, including the behavior of the owners of Robinhood, an online securities broker, and some members of the Wallstreetbets forum. However, we must first be on the same page regarding what ethical behavior is. Don't worry; we are not going to go into the boring philosophical meaning that can put you to sleep.

Merriam-Webster defines ethics in the following three ways:

- "The discipline dealing with what is good and bad and with moral duty and obligation."
- "A guiding philosophy."
- "The principles of conduct governing an individual or a group."

Based on the above definitions, the third definition of ethics relates closely with what we are interested in in this chapter. We want to explore if Robinhood ethically acted when they halted the buying of certain stocks during the GameStop short squeeze. Also, there were certain members of the Wallstreetbets forum who seemed to want to hurt some hedge funds which had shorted GameStop stock. Was their behavior ethical?

Ethics at its most basic level deals with classifying conduct as either good or bad. Now, who decides whether a certain behavior is good or bad, or ethical or unethical? In theory, no single individual does or should because whatever each person does affects others in some way or another. Hence, we have guidelines such as constitutions, codes of conduct, and policies and procedures. The assumption is that a person who participates in activities in places like stock markets must adhere to certain conducts and behaviors. Acting outside those guidelines may hurt others and possibly the industry. It is this sort of behavior we'll be investigating in this chapter.

A stock market is one of the places where participants should be treated equally. However, history in the United States financial markets suggests otherwise. One of the major issues facing market participants is conflict of interest. You have market makers such as Citadel investing in hedge funds such as Melvin Capital Management. There is no doubt that Melvin deals with brokers in its stock transactions. Is it not possible that the broker that Melvin uses sends their orders to Citadel for execution? Wouldn't there be a possible conflict of interest? Yes, it may not be direct because Citadel won't be dealing with Melvin directly. However, large investors tend to have closer relationships with their brokers and can influence them. From where I am sitting, a company that acts as a saver, investor, and investment advisor can easily mislead both the investing and trading public.

At the beginning of the GameStop short squeeze, Robinhood froze the buying of shares in certain stocks such as GameStop, Blackberry, AMC Entertainment Holdings, and Bed Bath & Beyond. Was this behavior by Robinhood ethical? To answer this question appropriately, we must find out more about Robinhood as a company. This means that we should investigate its history, how it operates, and most importantly, how it makes money.

Robinhood: The Uncommon Online Brokerage Firm

According to Robinhood's website, their mission is "to democratize finance for all." They went on to say, "We are proud to have created a platform that has helped everyday people, from all backgrounds, shape their financial futures and invest for the long term."

Furthermore, on their "About us" page, this online broker says, "At Robinhood, we believe the financial system should be built to work for everyone. That's why we create products that let you start investing at your own pace, **on your own terms** (emphasis is mine)." You cannot help but wonder whether what Robinhood says above is a marketing strategy or they meant it. I would expect them to have stood their ground to protect who they are. One of their values is transparency. Were they transparent with their customers when they stopped them from buying shares in GameStop and other stocks?

Let's go back to the founding of Robinhood to understand why they took a decision that helped hedge funds reduce their shorting losses. The company was founded by Baiju Bhatt and Vladimir Tenev when the United States and the rest of the world were recovering from the 2007-2008 financial crisis. The two met at Stanford University in 2005 as physics students. Both are sons of immigrant parents who had come to the United States to study for Doctor of Philosophy (Ph.D.) degrees.

Tenev went on to enroll in a Ph.D. program at the University of California, Los Angeles (UCLA). However, he decided to quit in 2011 and join Bhatt in building software for trading companies. In fact, they specifically built software tools for high-frequency traders who tended to be firms. At the time, the dust from Wall Street's 2010 "flash crash" had not yet settled. On May 6, 2010, the Dow Jones Industrial Average had dipped by about 1,000 points, and no one knew what had happened until after an investigation was done. The investigation pointed to high-frequency trading as the cause for the momentary plunge. The chart below shows the dip.

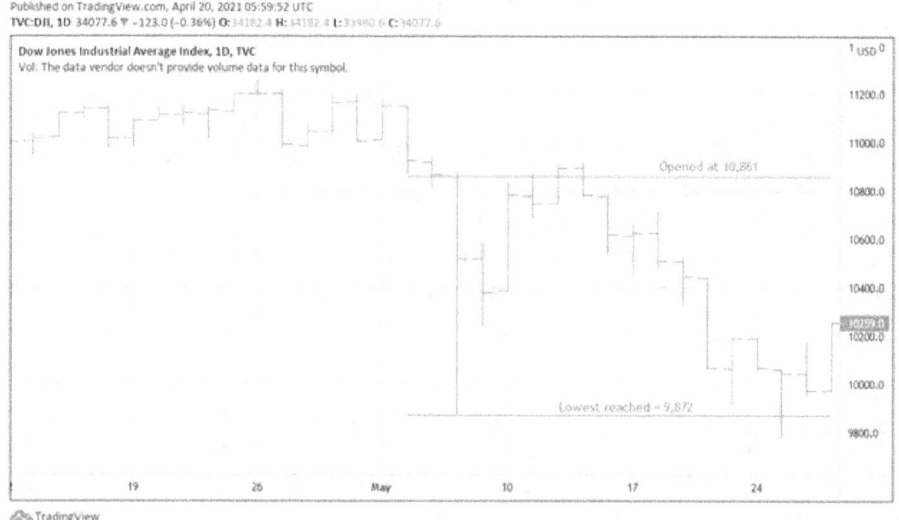

The events of that day were evidence that stock trading was shifting from traditional approaches to complex computer programs. This is one way that the stock market has created a huge gap between Wall Street and Main Street. It's not only stock trading that's affected—other markets are experiencing the same thing. High-frequency traders move within milliseconds to access orders ahead of traditional trading by institutions and retail investors. The latter ones are left to fight for the leftovers. In other words, the times heralded the introduction of new kings of Wall Street.

While Tenev and Bhatt were building software for high-frequency traders, they were getting insider knowledge in the operations of high-frequency trading. That way, they also learned how high-frequency traders made money. Tenev once told Mazarakis & Shontell (2017) on Business Insider that "All of the action happens in data centers, a lot of which are in New Jersey, and it's really about who has the fastest systems, the most automated systems, the best software. And those firms have an advantage when it comes to trading."

Remember that 2011 was also the year when the Occupy Wall Street movement raised concerns about unequal financial treatment between them and Wall Street firms. This event turned out to be a catalyst for Bhatt and Tenev to find a solution that would level the playing field in the financial markets, especially in trading and investing.

Here's how Tenev explained the inspiration of the Occupy Wall Street event this way: "A lot of people lost faith in the financial system, and it was becoming an insider game, and there were these sophisticated markets. Part of the reason was because hedge fund insiders had access to tools and resources that other people did not." He went on to say, "We were inspired to build something meaningful and something that empowered consumers" (Ongchoco, 2015).

Something else happened during the Occupy Wall Street event that caused Tenev and Bhatt to do some serious soul-searching. A friend of theirs accused them of benefiting from a financial system favoring only a few people but not the majority. The pair could not stomach the accusation and went on to think about how to be part of the solution and not the problem. That's when they conceived Robinhood, a mobile-friendly trading app. To further their mission, Tenev and Bhatt elected to forgo commissions and charge nothing on zero minimum balances. That was as disruptive to the industry as you can get at that time because giants like TD Ameritrade were making millions of dollars on commissions and other charges.

Robinhood was launched in 2013 but did not have the app yet. All they did was create a website with the intention of building a waiting list. They didn't think that the idea would work. However, by using a unique referral method, Robinhood had a waiting list of 1 million users by the time they launched their app on Apple's App Store in March 2015. In the initial round of funding, Robinhood raised $3 million from investors led by Index, Google Ventures, and Marc Andreessen, a software engineer, cofounder, and general partner of a venture capital firm known as Andreessen Horowitz.

How Robinhood Makes Money

Traditionally, brokers made money from commissions, among other charges. Now, if Robinhood doesn't charge commissions, how do they make money? This is an extremely important question in the context of Robinhood's action to halt buying of certain stocks during the GameStop short squeeze saga. Add to this the fact that Robinhood was charged $65 million for failing to disclose the exact sources of their income, and you have an interesting situation.

According to Jeff Kauflin and Antoine Gara of Forbes, Robinhood makes 70% of its revenue from payment for order flow (PFOF). In contrast, its competitors such as Schwab and E*TRADE earn 3% and 17% from PFOF, respectively. What is payment for order flow? Let's dive in and find out.

Payment for order flow is an income that a brokerage firm receives for directing orders to another firm for trade execution. In many cases, the firm that executes trades is a market maker. The amount a broker earns isn't much if you look at it on a per-share basis. However, when you consider that these firms forward thousands to millions of shares, you'll realize how significant PFOF can be.

PFOF is popular in the options market, and each contract traded can pocket a trader $0.50. This system of paying brokers was pioneered by Bernard Madoff, known for running the world's largest Ponzi scheme. A broker can receive fees for order flow without the knowledge of their clients. However, even if customers do know this, there is little chance they can stop any conflict of interest. What any retail investor should know is that their broker must disclose if they earn PFOF when you open an account with them. Furthermore, the broker must furnish such information annually.

According to Robinhood's fourth-quarter 2020 report on PFOF, they sent their customer orders to Citadel Execution Services, G1 Execution Services, Virtu Americas, and Wolverine Securities for both stocks and options (Robinhood, 2021). These are the firms to which Robinhood sends its customer orders for execution to earn 70% of its revenue. The remaining 30% is split in half between income from their gold membership subscriptions and lending of securities. So, Robinhood gets paid, not on the front-end in commissions, but on the back-end by selling trading orders to market makers. This strategy of free commissions is a powerful direct marketing technique that has been used for over 100 years.

The market makers, in turn, use their sophisticated trading systems to profit from securities' price spreads. Robinhood, unlike its competitors, does not charge market makers a fixed fee; instead, it charges a percentage of the spread. This means that the bigger the spread, the more Robinhood makes. It is clear that this strategy is not necessarily geared to give a Robinhood customer a good trading price for a security. In fact, it is possible that Robinhood may route their orders to a market maker who gives them the best price. That would be a firm that gets the most price spread. Sellers may benefit from this strategy, but buyers could purchase overpriced securities.

The online brokerage industry surged in 2020 amid the COVID-19 pandemic. Like other online brokerages, Robinhood made hay while the sun shone. Their PFOF income jumped from $91 million in the first quarter to $180 million in the second quarter. That's a rise of nearly 100%. Of this revenue, $111 came from options trading. This was fueled by an increase in trading volumes across the brokerage sector and an increase in Robinhood's funded accounts by 3 million new customers.

Why Robinhood Halted Buying Activity on January 28, 2020

Some brokers, including Robinhood, stopped retail investors and traders from buying GameStop shares and a few other stocks on January 28, 2021. Not only did Robinhood halt buy trading on GameStop stock, but they also increased margin requirements on selected securities. The decision followed after share prices in stock such as GameStop spiked and was accompanied by large trading volumes and volatility. Retail investors were furious with the decision because it blocked them from making more money. Some retail investors wanted the GameStop short squeeze to continue so that hedge funds could lose further millions on their short trades.

Under pressure to provide a plausible reason, Robinhood argued that they had stopped buying activity due to regulatory requirements. They went on to say that they acted that way not to please market makers as some people had suggested. Many other people were incensed by Robinhood's actions, including Alexandria Ocasio-Cortez, a House Representative from New York, and Senator Ted Cruz. Ocasio-Cortez came out strongly against Robinhood and said that there was a need to fully understand the online broker's decision. She accused Robinhood of blocking retail investors and allowing hedge funds to continue trading freely on both sides of the transaction. Unfortunately, she did not mention if hedge funds were trading on stocks affected by Robinhood's decision. Senator Ted Cruz agreed with Ocasio-Cortez that Robinhood had to explain their side of the story.

Let's now go into Robinhood's reasons for the above-mentioned decision. We first should understand the mechanics of a trade order fulfillment. An investor places a buy or sell order with their broker, who, in turn, transmits the order to an exchange such as the New York Stock Exchange. Market makers match buyers and sellers, and a transaction occurs if there is a match. As any retail investor can attest, the cash you get for selling a stock does not immediately become available for withdrawal after the trade. It takes one to two business days for you to access the money. Why is that the case?

In the old days, the time between completion of an order and access to cash was spent exchanging stock certificates between brokers. This process was practical in those days because trading volumes of stocks were low compared to today. In modern times, once a stock exchange executes a trade, it delivers the information to a private company called the Depository Trust & Clearing Corporation (DTCC). One of their subsidiaries is the National Securities Clearing Corporation (NSCC), which deals directly with Robinhood.

At any rate, a clearinghouse processes and completes a trade and helps limit transaction risk. They ensure that every trade happens whether a broker stays in business or not. In essence, the DTCC transfers stock ownership from a seller's broker to a buyer's broker and vice versa. The process is not completed after each trading day.

The DTCC waits for several trades to occur and processes them based on the order type per security, per client, per settlement date. A settlement date is the day on which cash and securities that are involved in a trade exchange hands. In other words, a seller's broker delivers the stock being traded, and the buyer's broker hands out the cash. It comes two days after an investor has traded. The DTCC receives a certain fee per trade.

For the DTCC to play their part, a broker must satisfy them that they have the assets necessary to complete a trade. You can think of these required assets as collateral. The size of the required collateral depends on the shares that are traded and their volatility. More stable stocks such as Amazon and Apple tend to have low collateral requirements because they are less risky for stock participants and the DTCC. Their collateral can be as low as 10% of the size of the transaction. Stocks such as GameStop had high volatility at the time in question and led to higher than normal collateral requirements.

According to Jeff Roberts on Fortune and a Nasdaq article, the NSCC required Robinhood to put forward $3 billion as collateral to process its trades. Fortune reports that Tenev, co-CEO of Robinhood, told Elon Musk on the Clubhouse app that Robinhood paid $1.4 billion in exchange for limiting trading in GameStop and other high-volatility stocks. It's surprising that the figure Robinhood paid is not the same across all sources. The Nasdaq article I mentioned above reported that Robinhood paid $700 million, which is half of what Fortune says was paid.

Even more astounding is the fact that Robinhood had the opportunity to set the record straight on one of their blogs on January 29, 2021. Instead, this is what they said, "The amount required by clearinghouses to cover the settlement period of some securities rose tremendously this week. How much? To put it in perspective, this week alone, our clearinghouse-mandated deposit requirements related to equities increased ten-fold." Do you remember I mentioned that one of Robinhood's values is transparency? Where is the transparency in this quote? Should we think that they were hiding something?

Tell me here, before today, had you ever heard about the DTCC? Few people have. Who owns the DTCC? A search on the internet brings unhelpful results. Yet, this is the company that claims to "stand at the center of the global trading activity, processing trillions of dollars of securities transactions on a daily basis" (Depository Trust & Clearing Corporation, n.d.). If I asked you who owns Apple, wouldn't you be able to tell me without hesitation? I am sure you would. Unfortunately, there is no easy answer regarding the DTCC.

According to its 2020 balance sheet, the DTCC has total assets worth $74.17 trillion. Its statement of income recorded $1.89 trillion in total revenue for the 2020 financial year.

How many companies do you know that have over a trillion in both assets and income? It is astonishing that few people are aware of this company. What you should take away from the DTCC information here is that it is a privately-held bank that serves institutions and brokerage firms only. Now, can this company actually bite the hands that feed it, such as Robinhood? There are many questions to ask about our financial system that would take several books to fully explain how it works.

The complexity of our financial system and lack of transparency are partly reasons the public barely has trust in it. As long as there is secrecy (sometimes in plain sight) in the true operation of the US financial system, average Americans are likely to stay skeptical about it. The GameStop short squeeze is exposing things that we never paid attention to in the past.

For example, the Robinhood co-CEO, Vladimir Tenev, is happy to simply tell his customers that the NSCC demanded $3 billion as collateral. Yet, he failed to disclose the numbers that he actually paid. So, Robinhood's investing customers should accept the explanation and move on as if nothing happened. However, are there no contingencies in Robinhood to help them manage such situations without hurting investors? Didn't they ever think that something like the GameStop buying activity could happen someday? As much as Robinhood must assume a certain level of blame, there is also an issue with the stock exchange system. Changing brokers won't help retail investors much because they'll face the same systematic issues with another online broker.

At any rate, Robinhood turned around the same day and allowed retail investors to buy a limited number of GameStop shares. It appears as if Robinhood's decision was to help let go of the squeeze so that hedge funds could cut their losses. However, the decision also impacted the incomes of some of the investors on the platform. In the final analysis, the financial system of the United States does not treat participants equally. The aggrieved parties may not sit back and watch as they suffer—they might find a way to revolt somehow.

Ethical Questions on the Wallstreetbets Forum Members

Questions have raised whether Wallstreetbets forum members ganged up to bring down certain hedge funds or not. We'll explore this concern below. For starters, Wallstreetbets forum members joined the subreddit with one major intention: "To make money as fast as possible." Furthermore, members share investment information that could be helpful for those who act on it. However, reading the posts and comments on the forum shows that some members have a gambling mentality. Still, there are other members who seem to want to hurt what some call "the big money."

In the lead-up to the GameStop short squeeze, it was clear that there were two types of investors in the stock. First, there were those who invested because they believed the GameStop stock was a bargain. They thought the company would bounce back, and they would benefit from its possible rising stock. The second type saw a chance to hurt hedge funds such as Melvin Capital Management and Citron. There is another group that joined the bandwagon when they realized there was an opportunity to make a quick buck.

It is the second group that I would like to focus on. The reason is that it is this group that could be accused of unethical practices. A post on Wallstreetbets that targeted any hedge fund was made on October 20, 2020, and the author was Stonksflyingup. It was titled "GME Squeeze and the Demise of Melvin Capital." This post attracted only 186 comments, and some comments came in while the short squeeze was on.

There were comments that clearly indicated that some of Wallstreetbets relished seeing Melvin Capital suffering. Here are a few for your own conclusion.

"Melvin has 40 million shares of luckin. They belong here." "This is the bedtime story I needed after yesterday and today, so thank you for this! I can't wait for your username to finally come true!" "I'm holding through what I think is the peak. I have an abusive relationship with GameStop. I'm willing to take only 5% profit to f***k bears trying to short this company."

There is no doubt Redditors mentioned above wanted hedge funds such as Melvin Capital to suffer from a short squeeze. However, did these members of Wallstreetbets have the means to push GameStop's stock to proportions causing a short squeeze? Also, you have to wonder whether these people bought enough shares to cause the short squeeze. All we can prove here is that there was an intention to take part in unethical behavior. It is not immediately apparent why the above Redditors wanted to see Melvin Capital suffering.

Part 3

Chapter 9: The Hearings and What the Future Holds for the Market and Retail Investors

The GameStop short squeeze has created challenges for regulators, brokers, market makers, investment fund managers, and retail investors. There is no doubt that many retail investors who bought GameStop stock near its peak have suffered big losses due to its volatility. However, retail investors who bought low prior to the start of 2021 and early in 2021 have reaped the rewards. At the same time, certain gaps within the US financial market have become apparent. One major shortcoming is the legal revenue-generating process we covered earlier, called payment for order flow. It is, therefore, essential that actions are taken to find out what really happened in this GameStop stock saga. One such step was the hearing by the US House Financial Services Committee.

The hearing was titled, "Game Stopped? Who Wins and Loses When Short Sellers, Social Media, and Retail Investors Collide." Maxim Waters, Committee Chairwoman, made a statement that captures the mood amongst retail investors when she said, "The market volatility surrounding GameStop has highlighted how many people feel that the cards are stacked against them." The first hearing took place on February 18, 2021, and the second occurred on March 17, 2021.

We'll begin with what transpired during the first hearing. The major participants invited were:

- Vladimir Tenev, CEO of Robinhood
- Gabriel (Gabe) Plotkin, CEO of Melvin Capital Management
- Steve Huffman, CEO and cofounder of Reddit
- Keith Gill, an individual investor
- Kenneth Griffin, CEO of Citadel
- Jennifer Schulp, director of financial regulation studies at Cato Institute

I'll provide a brief overview of the testimony that each of the above witnesses gave. I'll also make commentaries where necessary. As we proceed, you may make certain judgments that could be right or otherwise. That's absolutely fine because it is important to make your own judgments as this skill is essential for successful investing and trading.

Testimony by Gabriel Plotkin, CEO of Melvin Capital

Management

Gabriel Plotkin wasted no time in stating that his firm never took part in Robinhood's decision to halt certain trading on GameStop and other 'meme' stocks. He did this to shoot down any ideas that hedge funds may have influenced Robinhood in that decision. Plotkin informed the Committee that by the time Robinhood exercised their decision to halt some trading, Melvin had already closed their shorts a few days earlier.

Around that time, Citadel had invested a few billion in Melvin. Some commentators had thought that the money was to help Melvin close out their positions. However, Plotkin made it clear that Melvin did not need any cash injection despite having faced difficult times. He believed Citadel had seen an investment opportunity and wanted to take advantage. It is interesting that Plotkin did not say anything about Point72's $750 million cash injection.

I guess he didn't see the importance of mentioning it. However, Melvin announced both Citadel and Point72's investment in the same press release. The public has a right to think the money was a bailout owing to such events common on Wall Street.

Plotkin shifted his attention to an investment strategy that Melvin uses in selecting companies to invest in. According to Plotkin, here is the process Melvin follows.

- They focus their investments in companies that operate within the consumer and technology industry where GameStop takes part.

- Melvin mostly takes long positions in companies that they believe are growing through creating new products for their consumers, creating jobs, and contributing to economic growth. At the forefront of their search for these companies, Melvin digs deeper into the fundamentals of the business. Furthermore, Plotkin said, this research could take years to complete.

    If their research points that a company is overvalued, they short it for the long term. In addition, Melvin shorts stocks when the market is declining. Regarding shorting stocks, Plotkin had this to say, "In addition, it is very important to understand that absolutely none of Melvin's short positions are part of any effort to artificially depress or manipulate downward the price of a stock" (Plotkin, 2021). Perhaps the most important revelation was that Melvin had shorted GameStop since around 2014 because they believed (and still believe) that the company's business model was outdated and would fail it.

One thing that I believe Plotkin omitted was telling the Committee what hedge funds like his do after making certain investments. It is well-known that hedge funds often go out and tell others and the media about some of their investment decisions. Why they do that, I cannot tell. Now, when a fund comes out in the media and talks about their positions in certain stocks, would that not influence retail investors and possibly other fund managers?

Plotkin claimed that some Reddit participants began to make posts about Melvin's specific investments. You'll remember that Melvin has to file their investment positions with the SEC quarterly. That's the source where he may have believed Redditors obtained information about their short position on certain stocks. At any rate, he went on to say that Reddit members encouraged each other to take the opposite positions to Melvin's. It's clear here that Plotkin believes that retail investors ganged against his firm. Unfortunately, he could not provide numbers of such kinds of people for anyone to gauge their influence on the GameStop stock.

He went on to claim that some members of Reddit hurled insults and racist and profane messages in his direction. One such post apparently said, "It's very clear we need another holocaust; the Jews can't keep getting away with this." Then, he went on to explain that GameStop began to rise from $17 and peaked at $483 when ordinary investors bought its stock en masse. He said they closed their short positions in GameStop at a loss and also decreased their holdings in some other stocks due to the Reddit posts mentioned above.

I am extremely disappointed with the quality of the testimony that Plotkin gave in such a serious issue. He didn't tell the Committee that he had short GameStop stock via put options. Why didn't Melvin borrow shares directly if he strongly believed that GameStop was overvalued? I feel the testimony lacked facts to back up most of his claims.

It is interesting that Citadel, a market maker and a fund manager, invests in a hedge fund. They surely must have studied the business and agreed with its investment strategy. A bit more transparency could help in these transactions, and the timing of Citadel's investment in Melvin is also interesting. Why was this investment made at the time when Melvin was facing challenges? Plotkin should know that as long as he does not live by the integrity he claims Melvin subscribes to, there are going to be allegations, and some of them may be wrong.

Kenneth Griffin's Testimony

The next testimony we will go through was given by Kenneth Griffin, who founded Citadel and Citadel Securities. Like Plotkin, he absolved his firm in Robinhood's decision to stop buy trading on GameStop stock on January 28, 2021. One thing he also made clear was that Citadel is the largest market maker in the US equities market. This means that many brokers send their trades to Citadel Securities for execution. Furthermore, Griffin said that Citadel is an investment manager for pension plans, research institutions, and university endowments amongst its clients.

Griffin founded Citadel Securities 2002, a technology leader in transforming the market's infrastructure, especially for retail investors. The company carries out the market making process for the efficient operation of a stock exchange. Retail brokers like Robinhood charge market makers a fee to execute their retail trades. We have covered this fee (called PFOF) earlier, and we'll return to it shortly. Griffin believes that PFOF helps reduce investment costs and allows many Americans to invest.

It seems to me that Griffin was there to tout how good Citadel Securities is in market making. He suggested a few things that could be done to improve the efficiency of the market. One of the suggestions he put forth was to reduce the settlement days from two to one day. In addition, he argued that transparency at the clearinghouses would enable brokers and market makers to minimize the risk of market interruptions.

It's interesting that Griffin said nothing in his written testimony about his investment in Melvin Capital and whether it doesn't lead to a conflict of interest. One Committee member wanted to know whether retail investors get the best prices when using PFOF. Griffin kept avoiding answering the question directly. I previously explained how Robinhood charges market makers for its order flow. They charge them based on a percentage of the pricing spread. The higher the spread, the more money they make. Market makers want to get the highest spread they can get. So, market makers and Robinhood make the most money when retails pay more. That makes Robinhood's business of free commissions questionable. Does it serve investors or Robinhood?

Keith Gill's Testimony

You'll remember Keith Gill when we looked at what led to the GameStop short squeeze. We are not going to repeat what we said at that time. Rather, we will focus on some things we did not know about him and were relevant for the hearing. Gill prefaced his testimony by saying the following:

- He is not a hedge fund, does not have clients, and does not offer investment advice to anyone for a fee.

- He is an individual investor, invested in the GameStop stock, and made posts on social media regarding his investments in this video game retailer.
- He did not encourage or entice anyone into buying or selling a stock so he could profit.
- He was not part of any group that tried to push up the price of any particular stock.
- He never benefited or had any financial relationship with a hedge fund.
- He used public information on GameStop to make his investments, knew no one inside the company, and never spoke to an insider within the company.

With that out of the way, let's dig into the real testimony. Gill said that he uses public information to research the market and the value of companies he identifies. Using several factors, he keeps an eye on several stocks to identify investment opportunities. He said that he sometimes posts his analyses on individual stocks on social media. He believes doing so helps him identify where he may be getting things wrong. So, he analyzed GameStop, thought it was undervalued, and posted his thoughts on social media. There is no doubt that Gill believed that the market analyses given by financial experts were wrong.

Then, Gill went into his background for the Committee to decide whether he could be a person behind the GameStop short squeeze. In a nutshell, Gill was raised in Brockton, Massachusetts. His father was a truck driver, while his mother was a registered nurse. He was the first member of the family to obtain a four-year college degree. His first job was with W.B. Mason, an office supplying company, where he worked in operations.

Thereafter, he joined a start-up company owned by a family friend. He worked at this company between 2010 and 2014. While there, they tried to build software intended to help investors to analyze stocks. Again, they tried to start an investment firm but failed to make it work, and it failed soon after. It is here where Gill claims to have obtained some investing education. The most important education he believes he got concerns researching a company, including ferreting for facts in its financial statements. As part of his research process, he was taught to focus on a company's real long-term value, not on what gossip and news headlines say. Can you see some parallel between Michael Burry's and Gill's investment approach here? I hope that you do.

After marrying in 2016, Gill found a job at LexShares. I presume this company invests in commercial lawsuits and operates from Boston, Massachusetts. Here, he worked in operations. It is interesting that Gill does not specify the exact role or position he held at LexShares. At any rate, he left this company in March 2017 and stayed relatively unemployed for the next two years. That's when he began to actively analyze numerous stocks to buy and make a living and also as a passion.

Gill started working for MassMutual in April 2019 as director of financial wellness education. He and his wife were excited about the prospect because he had never had a salary of $100,000. Gill's main function at MassMutual was to develop financial education classes for use by advisors when presenting to prospective clients. He made sure to clarify that he was not a financial advisor, as some had suggested in the media, nor sold securities.

Meanwhile, he continued to analyze stocks during his spare time and also invested his family's money. GameStop came on his investment radar as a potential stock in June 2019. In the same month, June 7, to be exact, Gill bought GameStop stock's call options. I won't detail the rest of the developments of this investment since we have already covered the details elsewhere in this book.

Gill went on to say, "I want to pause to make a note that the investment I made was risky, but I was confident in my analysis, and I was willing to accept the loss if I was proven wrong. My timing was far from perfect, and many of the options contracts I purchased expired worthless because GameStop's stock price remained depressed longer than I expected."

The man who goes by the name Roaring Kitty on YouTube refuted claims that he used social media to attract investors to the GameStop stock. He argued that his focus was on the fundamentals of the business. To prove that he didn't drive people to the GameStop stock, Gill said that the largest audience he had on his streaming was 96. On average, these viewers stayed for about 25 minutes. He went on to say that on the morning of Christmas (I'm guessing in 2020), he had 529 subscribers on his YouTube channel and 550 followers on his Twitter account (Gill, 2021). You can make your own judgment as to whether Gill could be pointed out as the catalyst for the GameStop short squeeze.

Nearing the end of his testimony, Gill made an astounding statement and one that I believe is true. Let me quote him: "It's alarming how little we know about the inner workings of the market, and I am extremely thankful that this Committee is examining what happened." The key phrase to me is this "how little we know about the inner workings of the market." Now, who is responsible for ensuring that everyone knows the behind-the-scenes working of the stock market? The biggest challenge to addressing this problem is our denial to learn. We tend to prefer to reap the rewards without doing the necessary work.

In conclusion, Gill says he believed that understanding what actually happened in the GameStop short squeeze should begin with discovering the insanely high short interest in GameStop and potential manipulative short selling practices.

There you are. Use your judgment to decide whether you believe the media for picking out Keith Gill as the catalyst of the GameStop short squeeze or not.

I now move on to another testimony in the first hearing before discussing a key point I want to touch on from the second hearing.

CEO of Robinhood Vladimir Tenev's Testimony

Vladimir Tenev repeated most of what we talked about in the previous chapter when learning about Robinhood as a company. So, I am not going to waste your time with those details. Instead, I want to focus more on Robinhood's business model that depends on payment for order flow. Although we covered this subject earlier, there is more that I believe you should know.

The only new thing that you should take from Tenev's testimony pertains to what he thought could be done to avoid market interruptions similar to what his company did. He said this: "The industry, Congress, regulators, and other stakeholders need to come together to deploy our intellectual capital and engineering resources to move to real-time settlement of US equities." It's clear that he was echoing what Citadel's founder said. In short, Robinhood believes the design of the system made Robinhood decide to temporarily halt the buying of GameStop shares. This means there was nothing that his business could have done to prevent the event.

However, follow-up questions regarding his company's business model and customer service revealed flaws that need quick attention. Regarding customer service, US Representative Sean Casten illustrated how inadequate customer service was at Robinhood. Casten seemed to believe that it was poor customer service that may have led to Alex Kearns taking his life after mistakenly thinking he lost $730,000 on Robinhood's app. Representative Casten played the customer support line's message that said, "Thanks for calling Robinhood! Please visit us at Robinhood.com or our app for support. If you have an urgent need, please make sure to include details of your order when reaching out."

That was just the beginning of a long day for Tenev. One of the issues he was grilled on concerned how Robinhood makes money. As explained in the previous chapter, Robinhood uses an old direct marketing tactic of getting new customers or clients. The strategy works well by offering customers something they want for free. This is called the front end. Immediately a customer gives their contact details or enters the sales system, the back-end kicks in by selling targeted products or services to these people.

This is similar to the business model of companies like Facebook and several media companies. Facebook lures you into its ecosystem and, in turn, sells your information to advertisers. Robinhood attracts its customers, and they sign up, followed by making trades that the company hands over to market makers for cash. Yet, they claim that they don't charge commissions and fees for zero balances.

It's a good idea to bring in testimony from Sal Arnuk, cofounder of Themis Trading, who gave his side of the story during the second round of hearings. Arnuk focused almost exclusively on Robinhood's major cash-generating activity and the payment for order flow practice. In concluding his testimony, Arnuk said:

> The meme stock phenomenon in the markets today results from the dangerous intersection of poor investor education by some brokers and the PFOF practices that exist on and off stock exchanges. These practices create a massive incentive for such brokers to sell their clients' orders to sophisticated trading firms uniquely tooled to profit off of them. This is a needless conflict that can harm retail investors, and it degrades the integrity of the market ecosystem as a whole.

Based on the hearings so far, it seems an alternative to PFOF should be found so that retail investors get fair prices when investing.

Conclusion

We have now reached the end of *A Financial System Broken by Design*. I have no doubt you have learned many things along the way, and you'll approach your investments and trades with more awareness. Doing so would enable you to make informed investment decisions and protect yourself from losses.

Now, human beings have a tendency to forget what they learn. For that reason, we all could do with some reminding once in a while. The content you have read above is extremely important, and it should be internalized. The most effective way of keeping these ideas in your mind is through repetition. I don't need to convince you that this is true. Just refer back to how you learned in school, and you'll understand what I mean. I don't want you to forget what we covered above.

As a result, I am presenting you with key points that we covered together from the beginning to the end of the book. This summary will serve as a resource for you to reference when you need reminding. You can read it at least once a week to percolate the main ideas in your fertile mind.

We began the book by dealing with the US financial system. Investing occurs within the broader financial system. This financial system has many parts that are interconnected for it to work for all the participants. The reason a financial system exists is to connect savers with borrowers. Therefore, you are an important part of the financial system.

The other major parts of the US financial system include financial assets, financial institutions, financial markets, the SEC, and the Federal Reserve System. Financial assets are tradable securities such as stocks and bonds. These securities are sold in either primary or secondary financial markets. Most investors participate in secondary markets where holders of securities sell them to new owners. Accessibility to primary markets is limited because the major players tend to look for investors they know. This is one of the major talking points when the subject of an unequal financial system comes up.

Financial institutions are the intermediaries between savers and investors. The most common financial institutions are commercial banks, insurance companies, and hedge funds. Only accredited investors are allowed to become partners in hedge funds. An accredited investor earns at least $200,000 per year or has a net worth of over $1 million. Investment banks are responsible for helping companies join a stock market and also participate in mergers and acquisitions. The SEC acts as a regulator in the financial markets, especially the bond and stock markets.

A stock market is a financial market where private companies go to raise money for various reasons, such as ramping up their operations. In the process, investors participate in the stock market to grow their money. When a private company joins a stock market, it ceases to be a private business and becomes a public company. This means that it makes many aspects of its operations, such as its financial affairs, known to the public.

The process by which a company joins a stock market is called an initial public offering. Most investors at this stage are often institutions such as hedge funds. Investment banks ensure that a company succeeds in listing on a stock exchange. In the process, they may be paid a fee or in stocks. Once a company is listed, its shares are traded or bought and sold.

The major players in the stock market include stockbrokers, portfolio managers, custodian and depot service providers, and market makers. The latter ensures that orders reaching a stock market are executed, and they make money from the security's price spread. The bigger the spread, the more money they make. This is a hot issue because it can lead to a conflict of interest.

Investors use fundamental analysis to identify companies that are good investment prospects. The process is used to find undervalued businesses. Technical analysis is a tool commonly used by short-term traders. It helps forecast the future price of a stock and to time entry into the market.

One of the most important subjects we covered was about shorting a stock. Stock prices rise and also go down. Most investors choose to invest for appreciation. This means they buy at a low price and expect to sell at a higher price and pocket the difference after paying costs. However, sometimes the market enters into a bear phase where stock prices are in a general decline. Sophisticated investors and speculators are able to make money during this declining phase.

They do that by shorting stocks. This means that they borrow shares from their broker, sell them immediately, and hope the stock price declines further. Once it does, they buy the same number of shares and return them to a broker, and pocket the difference. The number of shares that are short in a stock indicates short interest. In other words, it gives an indication of the level of bearish sentiment on the particular stock. The higher the short interest, the more investors tend to think the affected stock will decline. However, the investment can turn into a loss if the stock's price rebounds and rallies upwards.

Forty-eight percent of American adults believe that the stock market is rigged. In other words, they believe that the odds are stacked against them making money in the stock market. It could be possible considering that there are some stocks where ownership is about 71% held by institutional investors. It's far easier for these people to band up and manipulate the stock than the retail investors can do.

The case of Athena, a high-frequency trading firm, provides evidence of stock market rigging. We know that the SEC charged the company for its role in manipulating the stock market. You'll recall that we covered the story of Kamilla Bjorlin, an actress from Hollywood. She had hired writers to pen glowing articles about certain companies she was doing stock promotion for. In the process, she broke some of the SEC rules and was charged nearly $750,000 for her troubles.

We started discussing short squeezes in Part 1, Chapter 5. The major short squeezes that we covered spanned the better part of the last 100 years of stock market history. The story of Piggly Wiggly® showed us that during a short squeeze, Wall Street finds a way to break it. If it means changing the rules, they will do it to protect short sellers. It was pretty clear that the retail investor and ordinary citizens are not considered very important in the stock market. Their importance only shows when contributing money to the market through vehicles like mutual funds and pension funds.

Two other short squeezes we covered were the Volkswagen and Tesla squeezes. Porsche had bought over 70% of Volkswagen shares while there were many short sellers in the stock. The squeeze happened when Porsche revealed their shareholding in Volkswagen. We concluded our discussion on short squeezes with the Tesla stock. The Tesla stock is considered one of the most shorted. Its price rallied to tremendous heights amid negative analysts' views. Many hedge funds had to close their positions to limit losses. However, the short squeeze never reached the proportions of the GameStop one, although it cost hedge funds a lot of money.

The discussion on the GameStop short squeeze started when we investigated GameStop, the company. We traced its origins because it was the major player in the whole short squeeze saga. A big takeaway from that study was that the company's stock began to perform poorly from around 2015. GameStop's net income became negative in 2018 and 2019. That's probably one of the reasons it attracted a large short interest.

Hedge funds claimed that they short the stock massively because they saw it running a flawed business model. They believed that GameStop would lose its business to online-based competitors.

We then investigated how the actual GameStop short squeeze happened and who the main role players were. The first investor who took a contrarian position to that held by short sellers was Michael Burry. The Scion Asset Management founder's investment strategy originated from the teachings of Benjamin Graham, the co-author of *Securities Analysis*. Burry clearly spelled out that his weapon of choice is research, and that's what he did with GameStop before investing in it.

The next important possible contributor was Keith Gill with his investment account posts on Reddit. He also shared his thoughts on GameStop on his YouTube channel. Gill argued that after researching the company, he decided to go long on its stock. Initially, few members of the Wallstreetbets forum where he shared his account status believed in his GameStop investment. However, Gill held on until the short squeeze happened.

The most important event that gave retail investors faith in GameStop was the appointment of Ryan Cohen and two other directors to the board of GameStop. That was on January 11, 2021, and soon after, the GameStop stock soared. It had been increasing gradually from around August 2020 following Ryan Cohen's announcement that he bought around 9.98% stake in GameStop.

In the last two chapters, we turned our attention to possible unethical behaviors of Robinhood and some members of Wallstreetbets. Based on our definition of ethical behavior, we found that Robinhood not only acted unethically but it also went against its own values, such as transparency. In studying Robinhood, we found that it gets nearly 70% of its revenue from payment for order flow. The latter is the practice of routing orders to market makers for payment. Robinhood sends its customers' orders to market makers such as Citadel, Two Sigma, and two other companies.

We also found that some members of Wallstreetbets acted unethically when they targeted to hurt Melvin Capital for reasons that were not clear. But responses to the Wallstreetbets post titled "GME Squeeze and the Demise of Melvin Capital" showed the intent to cause damage. Was this a fair practice? Definitely not.

The subsequent hearings that took place on February 18 and March 17, 2021, centered around establishing what transpired that led to the GameStop short squeeze. The House also wanted to know why Robinhood halted the buying of shares in Robinhood on January 28, 2021. The major issue established was Robinhood's way of generating revenue. Several questions were raised around its payment for order flow income steam and potential conflict of interest.

Going forward, it is likely that the payment for order flow system might be eliminated. As far as each individual investor is concerned, the onus should be on each one to perform due diligence when choosing brokers and when investing. Finance is a thinking game, and any investor should play the game with care.

I believe every investor has a duty to understand how our financial system works to make sound and ethical decisions. Trying to prove a point will not get us anywhere except to argue against one another. I hope this book has opened your eyes to some of the things that might not have been clear in the past.

References

[DeepF***gValue]. (2020, October 8). *GME YOLO update — Oct 8 2020 [Online forum]*. Reddit. https://www.reddit.com/r/wallstreetbets/comments/j7ki10/gme_yolo_update_oct_8_2020/

[Senior_Hedgehog]. (2021, January 30). *Update: GME - Biggest short squeeze of your life from 9 months ago [Online forum]*. Reddit. https://www.reddit.com/r/wallstreetbets/comments/l8dfiy/update_gme_biggest_short_squeeze_of_your_life/

[Stonksflyingup]. (2020, October 28). *GME squeeze and the demise of Melvin Capital. [Online forum post]*. Reddit. https://www.reddit.com/r/wallstreetbets/comments/jjctxg/gme_squeeze_and_the_demise_of_melvin_capital/

Arnuk, S. (2021, March 17). *Thank you esteemed members of the House Financial Service Committee for inviting me to participate in this hearing*. U.S. Committee on Financial Services. https://financialservices.house.gov/uploadedfiles/hhrg-117-ba00-wstate-arnuks-20210317.pdf

Board of the Federal Reserve System. (2020, August 27). *The Fed - Why does the Federal Reserve aim for 2 percent inflation over time?* Board of Governors of the Federal Reserve System. https://www.federalreserve.gov/faqs/economy_14400.htm

Brooks, J. (2014). *Business adventures*. Open Road Integrated Media, Inc.

Burry, M. (2001). *MSN Money articles*. csinvesting. http://csinvesting.org/wp-content/uploads/2013/07/Michael-Burry-Case-Studies.pdf

Capital, N. (2019, August 20). Shorting GameStop is a dangerous game. *Seeking Alpha*. https://seekingalpha.com/article/4286973-shorting-gamestop-is-dangerous-game

CFI. (n.d.). *2 and 20 - How the 2 and 20 hedge fund fee structure works*. Corporate Finance Institute. https://corporatefinanceinstitute.com/resources/knowledge/trading-investing/2-and-20-hedge-fund-fees

Chen, J. (2021, January 24). *Hedge fund definition*. Investopedia. https://www.investopedia.com/terms/h/hedgefund.asp

Cohen, R. (2020). *Maximizing stockholder value by becoming the ultimate destination for gamers*. Securities and Exchange Commission. https://www.sec.gov/Archives/edgar/data/1326380/000101359420000821/rc1 3da3-111620.pdf

Depository Trust & Clearing Corporation. (n.d.). *About DTCC*. DTCC. https://www.dtcc.com/about

Dusaniwsky, I. (2021, January 26). *GameStop shorts down $5 billion in 2021*. S3 Shortsight. https://www.shortsight.com/gamestop-shorts-down-5-billion-in-2021/

FinancialWeb. (n.d.). *Primary vs secondary bond markets*. FinancialWeb. https://www.finweb.com/investing/primary-vs-secondary-bond-markets.html

GameStop. (n.d.). *Ownership summary*. GameStop. https://news.gamestop.com/stock-information/institutional-ownership

GameStop. (2020, March 26). *2019 annual report*. GameStop. https://news.gamestop.com/static-files/9d2139e1-31c7-498f-ad95-63db1e6d085a

Gill, K. P. (2021, February 18). *Testimony of Keith Patrick Gill before the United States House of Representatives Committee on Financial Services*. U.S. House Committee on Financial Services. https://financialservices.house.gov/uploadedfiles/hhrg-117-ba00-wstate-gillk-20210218.pdf

GTS. (n.d.). *Home*. GTS. https://gtsx.com/

Hallam, J. (2019, August 20). *Scion Asset Management urges GameStop to buy back $238 million of stock with cash on hand*. Businesswire. https://www.businesswire.com/news/home/20190819005633/en/Scion-Asset-Management-Urges-GameStop-Buy-238?mod=article_inline

Hebron, J. (2020, January 8). *Size of U.S. mortgage market in 2020 (January edition)*. Finance.yahoo.com. https://finance.yahoo.com/news/size-u-mortgage-market-2020-154148225.html

Inflation Tool. (n.d.). *Value of 2008 euro today - Inflation calculator*. Inflation Tool. https://www.inflationtool.com/euro/2008-to-present-value?amount=400

Intrado GlobeNewsWire. (2021, January 11). *GameStop announces additional board refreshment to accelerate transformation.* Intrado GlobeNewsWire. https://www.globenewswire.com/news-release/2021/01/11/2156168/0/en/GameStop-Announces-Additional-Board-Refreshment-to-Accelerate-Transformation.html

Isidore, C. (2021, January 6). *Tesla short sellers lost $40 billion in 2020. Elon Musk made more than triple that.* CNN Business. https://edition.cnn.com/2021/01/06/investing/tesla-shorts-losses-elon-musk-win/index.html

Kauflin, J., & Gara, A. (2020, August 19). *The inside story of Robinhood's billionaire founders, option kid cowboys and the Wall Street sharks that feed on them.* Forbes. https://www.forbes.com/sites/jeffkauflin/2020/08/19/the-inside-story-of-robinhoods-billionaire-founders-option-kid-cowboys-and-the-wall-street-sharks-that-feed-on-them/?sh=48d3430c268d

Kolakowski, M. (2021, March 17). *At $1 trillion, Apple is bigger than these things.* Investopedia. https://www.investopedia.com/news/apple-now-bigger-these-5-things/

Mazarakis, A., & Shontell, A. (2017, July 6). *The founders of Robinhood, a no-fee stock-trading app, were initially rejected by 75 venture capitalists — now their startup is worth $1.3 billion.* Business Insider. https://www.businessinsider.com/robinhood-app-vlad-tenev-founder-free-stock-trading-valuation-2017-7?IR=T).

Merriam-Webster. (n.d.). *Definition of ethic.* Merriam-Webster. https://www.merriam-webster.com/dictionary/ethic

Ongchoco, D. (2015, August 12). *Startup insider: The story behind stock trading app Robinhood and its one million-person waitlist.* HuffPost. https://www.huffpost.com/entry/startup-insider-the-story_b_7976446

Ortex. (n.d.). *Short interest and securities lending data for NYSE:GME.* Ortex. https://www.ortex.com/symbol/nyse/gme/short_interest

Plotkin, G. (2021, February 18). *Hearing before the United States House of Representatives Committee on Financial Services.* U.S. House Committee on Financial Services. https://financialservices.house.gov/uploadedfiles/hhrg-117-ba00-wstate-plotking-20210218.pdf

Porsche SE. (2008, October 26). *Porsche heads for domination agreement*. Porsche SE. https://www.porsche-se.com/en/news/press-releases/details/news/detail/News/porsche-heads-for-domination-agreement-1

Powell, J. (2018, October 31). *The day Volkswagen briefly conquered the world*. Financial Times. https://www.ft.com/content/0a58b63a-4294-3e07-8390-c3aabef39a26#comments-anchor

Roberts, J. J. (2021, February 3). *The real story behind Robinhood's decision to restrict GameStop trading—and that 4am call to put up $3 billion*. Fortune. https://fortune.com/2021/02/02/robinhood-gamestop-restricted-trading-meme-stocks-gme-amc-vlad-tenev-nscc/

Robinhood. (n.d.). *About us*. Robinhood. https://robinhood.com/us/en/about-us/

Securities and Exchange Commission. (2020). Final judgment as to defendant Kamilla Bjorlin. *Securities and Exchange Commission*. Securities and Exchange Commission. https://www.sec.gov/litigation/litreleases/2020/judgment24716-bjorlin.pdf

Statista. (2021, January 20). *Percentage added to U.S. GDP 2018, by industry*. Statista; Statista. https://www.statista.com/statistics/248004/percentage-added-to-the-us-gdp-by-industry/

Tenev, V. (2021, February 18). *Hearing before the United States House of Representatives Committee on Financial Services*. U.S. Committee on Financial Services. https://financialservices.house.gov/uploadedfiles/hhrg-117-ba00-wstate-tenevv-20210218.pdf

Uchitelle, L. (2009, January 9). U.S. lost 2.6 million jobs in 2008. *The New York Times*. https://www.nytimes.com/2009/01/09/business/worldbusiness/09iht-jobs.4.19232394.html

ValueWalk. (2020, February 18). *Michael Burry net worth*. ValueWalk. https://www.valuewalk.com/michael-burry-bio/

Wijman, T. (2020, May 8). *The world's 2.7 billion gamers will spend $159.3 billion on games in 2020; The market will surpass $200 billion by 2023*. Newzoo. https://newzoo.com/insights/articles/newzoo-games-market-numbers-revenues-and-audience-2020-2023/

XE Business. (2021, April 28). *Convert 467.34 EUR to USD*. XE Business. https://www.xe.com/currencyconverter/convert/?Amount=467.34&From=EUR&To=USD

www.ingramcontent.com/pod-product-compliance
Lightning Source LLC
Chambersburg PA
CBHW070416220526
45466CB00004B/1425